CANADA IN THE
CHANGING WORLD ECONOMY

B. W. Wilkinson
University of Alberta

CANADA-U.S. PROSPECTS
a series sponsored by
C. D. Howe Research Institute (Canada)
National Planning Association (U.S.A.)

Legal Deposit — 2nd Quarter 1980
Quebec National Library
Library of Congress Catalog Number 80-80329
ISBN 0-88806-067-X
April, 1980, $10

C. D. Howe Research Institute (Montreal, Quebec) and
National Planning Association (Washington, D.C.)
Printed in Canada

To
Myrna, Glenda,
Myrna-Lynn, and Craig

CONTENTS

v

FOREWORD

The Canadian economy is as full of anomalies as is Canada itself. Endowed with an unusually abundant natural resource base, especially in comparison with its relatively small population, Canada has long been regarded as having an exceptionally promising economic future. Since World War II this promise has in many respects been translated into reality. Nevertheless, nagging problems, many of which are viewed as quite serious by Canadian economists having a broad range of perspectives, continue to plague the country's performance. This study, the sixth to be released in the Canada-U.S. Prospects (CUSP) series, provides a detailed analysis of the growth and development of the Canadian economy over the past three decades and offers commentary on many of the policy issues that preoccupied Canadians during that period — and that continue to rank very highly in current political debate.

The author of this study, B. W. Wilkinson, is Professor of Economics at the University of Alberta in Edmonton. Dr. Wilkinson has established a reputation as both a careful researcher and an unconventional commentator on Canadian economic policy issues. A close personal friend, over the years he has challenged me on numerous occasions with novel views and insights. I have encouraged him to be equally challenging in this study, since his point of view differs from that of many other authors in the CUSP series.

The bulk of this study parallels a study on the U.S. economy — the fifth volume released in this series — by Solomon Fabricant. While Dr. Wilkinson's methodology is somewhat different than Dr. Fabricant's, the two studies taken together provide effective diagnoses of the U.S. and Canadian economies at the beginning of the 1980s. An integration of these two nationally focused investigations for purposes of examining the bilateral implications of their findings will be undertaken in the concluding volume of this series.

Dr. Wilkinson casts his net much more broadly than does Dr. Fabricant, especially in his final chapter and in an extended appendix on proposals for Canadian-U.S. free-trade arrangements. The points he raises concerning economic policy issues relating to Canada, including the issue of the bilateral relationship, merit the attention particularly of those in the United States who have been expressing renewed interest in that country's relations with Canada. Dr. Wilkinson's perspective — one widely shared in Canada — is that, while the bilateral relationship has brought many benefits to Canada, numerous domestic initiatives are required before the opportunities that a free-trade arrangement might bring can be sought within acceptable limits of economic and political risk.

Most of the data used in this study are for the period up to 1978. Developments over the past year serve to confirm, in Dr. Wilkinson's mind, the conclusions reached in his study.

Carl E. Beigie
Series Coordinator

ACKNOWLEDGMENTS

I am greatly indebted to Carl Beigie for the many valuable discussions I was able to have with him prior to, and over the course of, preparing this study; for his encouragement; and for his detailed comments on earlier drafts of this paper. Without his assistance in these and other ways, this study would never have reached this final stage. He is, however, to be absolved from those weaknesses or omissions that remain. And, of course, the conclusions and recommendations submitted are not always the ones he would necessarily agree with.

I am also grateful to my typists, Maria Figueroa and Celeste Best, for their efficient and careful transformation of my rough papers into readable form. Maria cheerfully bore the brunt of the seemingly constant stream of changes that I made in the course of pulling everything together.

The contributions of other members of the C. D. Howe Research Institute who provided assistance in a variety of ways as this study was in progress were important, too, in bringing it to a conclusion. Finally, the financial support of the foundations making the Canada-U.S. Prospects series possible is appreciatively acknowledged.

1

Introduction

The period since World War II has been one of generally rapid economic growth and unparalleled prosperity for the developed nations of the Western world. But world production, international payments balances, and exchange rates have undergone major fluctuations over the past several years.[1] These fluctuations have included

- the U.S. balance of payments crisis of 1971, culminating in the formal suspension of dollar convertibility in August of that year;
- the surge in world output in 1972 and especially in 1973, coupled with pressure on existing capacity, crop failures, food shortages, and concomitant inflation accommodated by permissive monetary policy;
- a new U.S. exchange crisis in the first quarter of 1973, resulting in a shift to a floating-exchange-rate system by the United States and a number of other major countries, followed by recurring erosion in the international currency value of the U.S. dollar and substantial swings in the values of other industrial countries' currencies vis-à-vis one another;
- the oil crisis in the autumn of 1973 and the subsequent massive rise in the OPEC oil price;
- the severe anti-inflationary policies adopted by most major industrial nations in 1974 to reduce inflation, which in the process precipitated the most dramatic recession since World War II;
- more recent hesitant, and somewhat erratic, efforts to restore economic growth without stimulating new, more extreme inflation.

World trade has reflected these swings and shifts. It rose sharply, in terms of both value and volume, in 1973; dropped absolutely in volume in 1974-75; rose again in 1976; and slowed down in 1977-78.

---

[1] For a more extensive review of these fluctuations and the problems they have created and for some suggestions for coping with them, see Carl E. Beigie, *Inflation Is a Social Malady* (Montreal, Washington, D.C., and London: British-North American Committee, 1979).

1

The Tokyo Round of GATT negotiations has produced some reductions in trade barriers, to be instituted over the next eight years, but this by no means implies the end of developed nations' attemps to shelter their own production and labor forces from foreign competition at the same time that developing nations are becoming more adamant in their demands for an enlarged share of the world's material goods. Concurrent with a continuing desire on the part of individuals and societies to appropriate for themselves as large a portion as possible of the world's riches, many are raising concerns relating to environmental pollution, to the continuing population explosion in developing countries, and, more generally, to whether our planet can support continued world economic expansion of the type followed by the major advanced nations. There has also been a growing awareness that, in the Western world, improvements in material welfare have not reduced social and personal discontent, insecurity, fear, immorality, and violence.

Canada, for its part, is experiencing a high unemployment rate, substantial inflation, continued regional income and employment inequalities, considerable labor strife, and a large deficit on the current account in the balance of payments. To compound these difficulties, much doubt persists as to the availability of investment funds to meet the future "needs" of the economy, morale is low in the business community, and the possibility of Quebec's separating from the rest of the nation looms as a near-term threat.

This, then, is the context in which we wish to examine, in some detail, Canada's record of economic advance over the past two decades or so and, if possible, to gain a better understanding of the nation's potential. Such an examination will provide — along with a separate but broadly similar discussion of U.S. economic growth and potential by Solomon Fabricant[2] — a basis for pinpointing areas that may be of particular bilateral concern and require close attention in the future or, alternately, that may provide opportunity for greater cooperation between our two nations.

In Chapter 2 we present an overview of Canada's economic growth, focusing upon factors influencing the quantity and quality of the labor supply and upon the regional and industrial distribution of employment. This review will enable us to make a number of observations about what we can expect with regard to the labor component of growth.

In Chapter 3 we examine the augmentation of investment and capital stock, sources of savings, and issues of relevance for the future expansion of the economy.

---

[2] Solomon Fabricant, *The Economic Growth of the United States: Perspective and Prospective*, Canada-U.S. Prospects series (Montreal and Washington, D.C.: C. D. Howe Research Institute and National Planning Association, 1980).

After surveying labor and capital inputs, we turn our attention, in Chapters 4 and 5, to the major tradable-commodity-producing sectors of the economy — manufacturing and the resource industries — to consider specifically their development and the main problems they are now facing. In Chapter 6 we build on the previous two chapters and look at Canada's merchandise trade position over time, placing this performance in the broader context of the entire Canadian balance of payments. In Chapter 7 we provide a brief summary of the previous chapters and draw conclusions on the basis of the analysis there. In Chapter 8 we explore several options with respect to Canada's future international position in terms of their impact upon this country's productivity growth, economic advance in general, and relations with the United States. Four appendixes complete the study.

A few words of caution to the reader are necessary. It is pretentious to think of reviewing Canada's postwar economic development, outlining current problem areas, and suggesting several options in the space allowed for this study, although these were essentially the terms of reference for this study. Consequently, there are some topics not touched upon that the reader may think should have been; or if they are mentioned, they may not be developed to the reader's satisfaction. It has been necessary to be selective. Much could have been said, for example, about the burgeoning service sector. But because this sector produces primarily non-tradable commodities that neither earn nor cost foreign exchange or that, if traded, comprise a relatively small portion of the total trade and payments account,[3] little has been said about it. We wanted to concentrate upon those segments of the economy where the international economic environment, and particularly relationships with the United States, were of major importance. Similarly, details provided on, and discussion of, merchandise trade and international capital flows are relatively limited, for these too are discussed in other monographs in this series. Again, we could have devoted much more time to an analysis of the extension and significance of the government sector and its components. However, we restricted ourselves largely to mentioning certain issues relating to government contributions to savings and to government policies affecting commodity-producing industries. Finally, much more might have been said about interregional inequities and tensions and the Quebec separation issue; however, another series of studies focuses on these types of questions.[4]

---

[3] There are exceptions to this, of course, such as the entertainment industry in its broadest sense.

[4] See the publications in the C. D. Howe Research Institute's Accent Québec series (published between 1977 and 1980).

I

A BROAD OVERVIEW OF
CANADA'S ECONOMIC ADVANCE

2

Output Growth and Labor Input

Introduction

In this chapter we provide an overview of the identifiable influences contributing to expanded output in the economy and consider the extent to which these influences, particularly those relating to labor supply, will be important in Canada's economic advance.

Economic output depends upon the supply of the basic factors of production — labor, capital, and natural resources — and upon the efficiency with which they are combined. Efficiency is a function of such factors as the level of technology; the scale of operation; the quality of natural resources; the education and skill of management; the education, training motivation, initiative, and energy of the labor force; and the legal and human environment in which business has to operate. The potential growth rate of output depends upon the rates of growth of these factors.

Whether output reaches this potential depends upon the strength of demand for the goods and services produced. The components of this demand are government expenditures, consumer outlays, investment (in machinery and equipment as well as in residential and non-residential construction), and net exports (that is, after imports are deducted).

Actual and potential output are closely interdependent. Investment, for example, forms a portion of total demand, but it also expands the capital stock upon which future production depends. Again, while consumption adds to expenditures, it is also a motive for additional labor supply to be offered.

Although we shall be thinking primarily in terms of the contributions that the various factors of production (including their quality) and technological change have made to the growth of output in the past, it should always be borne in mind, even if not always stated, that behind these inputs there has had to be a level of demand sufficient to utilize them to the extent they have been utilized. In later chapters we shall return to the demand issue as we discuss the implications of supply, productivity, and factor-cost trends for future economic advance.

7

In statistical estimates of the components of output growth, the usual items listed as "explaining" such an advance are generally simplified from those mentioned above. The least elaborate format is to look at labor input and its productivity, where "productivity" is a basket category picking up the effects of perhaps a higher capital/labor ratio, the improved quality of labor and capital, and all other forces making for gains in output. A more elaborate estimation framework, usually referred to as the total-factor-productivity approach, provides for the enlargement of the supply of both labor and capital input (sometimes adjusted for quality changes), plus a measure of aggregate technological change (sometimes subdivided into such identifiable influences as changing scale economies and resource shifts among sectors and a residual "unexplained" contribution). The specific contribution of natural resource inputs and the influence of their varying qualities are not generally calculated separately because of statistical difficulties. Yet it would be useful to be able to quantify the effect of such factors as the exhaustion of high-quality, easily accessible ore bodies and other mineral reserves and the need to mine lower-quality, less accessible deposits. Also, knowledge of such factors as the effects on agricultural productivity of urban spread that reduces the availability of high-quality land would be worthwhile.

Omissions of this sort, however, are probably not too serious. Changing natural resource availability will be picked up in the form of a reduced rate of technological advance and/or perhaps by a higher capital/output ratio, since more capital must be invested to sustain or improve output growth. But we shall leave this and a variety of related topics to subsequent chapters. For now, we confine ourselves to the simplest approach to output growth and its determinants, which is based on the quantity of labor and the level of labor productivity.

The Past Record

Labor and Labor Productivity: Trends

With the exception of a few occasions, such as during the 1930s, Canada has enjoyed continuous economic growth ever since Confederation in 1867. Between 1867 and the end of 1977, gross national product (GNP), in constant 1971 dollars, expanded from about $2.2 billion to $123 billion, or by a multiple of approximately 56. The population also grew over the same period, from 3.5 million to 23.3 million, or by a factor of 6.6. Hence, in terms of material well-being — insofar as this can be measured by GNP — annual average income per person improved by a multiple of over 8.[1]

---

[1] Figures for 1867 are from O. J. Firestone, *Canada's Economic Development* (London: Bowes and Bowes, 1958), Tables 4 and 10, although GNP estimates have been inflated to 1971 constant dollars. Figures for 1977 are from Department of Finance, *Economic Review*, 1978 (Ottawa, 1978).

A little more detail on the growth record is provided in Table 1. Since the beginning of World War II, real economic expansion has been, on average, considerably faster than during the first six decades or so of Confederation. Growth was particularly outstanding during the war years themselves, following, as they did, the major world depression of the 1930s, when growth of total output in Canada was negligible and that of per capita output was negative. But even the period since the war has been one of remarkable growth by historical standards. This is especially evident from 1948 to 1974, the years of the earliest and latest business-cycle peaks for the period, when output expansion averaged 5.1 percent, compounded annually.

This long-run growth rate masks a number of cyclical fluctuations over the period examined. Some indication of these is provided in Table 1. The 1948-56 period, although it included a recession in 1953-54, was one of particularly strong advance, as a consequence of the Korean War in the early 1950s, the great resource development boom, and the construction of the St. Lawrence Seaway. The economy sagged badly from the beginning of the recession early in 1957 until the commencement of a sustained recovery in 1961. (Inappropriate monetary policies during this period attracted capital inflows and pushed the Canadian dollar much higher than it should have been, thereby worsening Canada's external competitive position. Consequently, the modest business-cycle peak in January, 1960, still left much idle capacity in the economy.) More recently, the world boom of the early 1970s had a favorable impact upon Canadian growth in 1969-74. The world recession and faltering recovery since 1973 are reflected in the much more modest Canadian total output gains in the 1973-78 period, although these gains are still quite reasonable compared with those of the pre-Great Depression years.

Growth in output per capita and in output per employed person (one measure of what is referred to as "labor productivity") has also been greater, on average, since World War II than in the pre-1929 period (see Table 1, columns 2 and 3). Over the past fifteen years the expansion in the number of workers has also been exceptional (see Table 1, column 4), surpassing even the great swell from 1900 to 1910, when net immigration was an outstanding contributor to labor force growth. In fact, since the 1974 business-cycle peak, the growth of additional labor input has been responsible for most of the increase in total output and output per person that has occurred. Productivity growth has been quite small — well below both post- and pre-World War II trends. (Near the top of the business cycle and during the initial stages of a downswing, it is quite normal for productivity growth to slow down and even to diminish. As an upswing commences, output per worker usually rises significantly as excess capacity is utilized. However, this expected improvement in productivity did not occur in 1973-78.)

TABLE 1

**Compound Annual Growth Rates of Gross National Output,
Output per Capita, and Output per Employed Person, 1867-1978**
(constant dollars)

Period	Gross National Output	Output per Capita	Output per Employed Person [a]	Growth of Output Owing to Expanded Labor Input [b]
	(1)	(2)	(3)	(4)
1867-1930	3.2	1.5	1.2	2.0
1867-1890	3.0	1.6	1.2	1.8
1890-1910	4.1	2.1	1.3	2.7
1910-30	2.6	.7	1.0	1.6
1929-45	3.5	2.3	2.7	.9
1929-39	.5	-.7	-.1	.7
1939-45	8.6	7.3	7.2	1.3
1946-78	4.8	2.7	2.3	2.5
Earliest to latest peak years in postwar period:				
1948-74	5.1	2.9	2.6	2.5
Selected subperiods, peak year to peak year: [c]				
1948-56	5.8	3.2	4.1	1.7
1956-59	2.8	0	1.1	1.7
1959-69	5.2	3.3	2.3	2.9
1969-74	5.3	4.0	1.9	3.4
Years since last major peak:				
1974-78	3.5	2.1	1.1	2.4

[a] For 1870-1930 the Armed Forces are included, whereas for 1929-78 only civilian workers are counted. These figures are not comparable with those in publications such as Statistics Canada, *Aggregate Productivity Measures, 1946-1977* (Ottawa, 1978), which considers only commercial industries and excludes government employees, educational institutions, and the like.
[b] Calculated independently but should also equal column 1 minus column 3. Where differences occur, it is because of rounding.
[c] The actual business-cycle periods were as follows:

Peak	Trough
1929 Q2	1933 Q1
1937 Q3	1938 Q4
n.a.	1946 Q1
1948 Q4	1949 Q3
1953 Q2	1954 Q3
1956 Q4	1958 Q3
1959 Q3	1961 Q1
1966 Q2	1968 Q1
1969 Q1	1970 Q4
1974 Q1	1975 Q2

n.a. = not available

Sources: 1867-1930: O. J. Firestone, *Canada's Economic Development, 1867-1953* (London: Bowes and Bowes, 1958), Table 11, p. 68.
1929-78: Statistics Canada, System of National Accounts, *National In-*

Finally, the fact that output per capita increased at a faster pace than that of output per employed person from 1959 to 1978 suggests that the number of persons of labor force age and/or labor-force-participation rates were rising.

With these broad trends in mind, let us examine in somewhat greater detail changes in the labor force and related magnitudes, with particular emphasis upon recent decades.

Population and Labor Force Growth

The most important source of labor force growth over the past decade or so has been the surge in birth rates during the fifteen years following World War II. Population growth rates were therefore particularly rapid during the 1950s (see Table 2(a), column 1), resulting in an increasing proportion of the population being of labor force age during the latter 1960s and early 1970s (see Table 2(b), column 4). This implies, in turn, that — even if participation rates for the various age groups of labor force age had remained unchanged — the labor force would have experienced more rapid growth than in earlier years.

Another major factor in the recent rapid expansion of the number of workers — accounting for 25-30 percent of the expansion — is that the overall participation rate has increased in all regions of Canada.[2] In 1951 it was about 53 percent of those persons at least 14 years of age; in 1977 it was 61.5 percent. This increase is the *net* result of two main trends:

• a modest decline in the labor-force-participation rate among males, at least since 1961 — particularly among those aged 65 and over and, to a lesser extent, among those aged 45-64 (the rates for 14-19- and 20-24-year-old groups also declined until about 1971, but since then have been rising again, thereby directly raising the total male participation rate once more);

• an enormous expansion in the participation rate among women of all ages, particularly married women — except those over 65 and, to a lesser extent, those under 20.

---

[2] Although regional differences persist, with such low-income regions as Quebec and, particularly, the Atlantic provinces having participation rates much lower than the national average — in 1977, 58.8 percent for Quebec and 53.8 percent for the Atlantic provinces versus 61.5 percent for Canada (see the figures for labor-force-participation rates in Table 4).

TABLE 2

Population and Labor Force Changes, 1951-78

(a) Population and Labor Force Increases, 1951-78

		Percentage Increase			Net Immigration As % of Total Labor Force Increase
		Labor Force			
	Population	From Domestic Sources	From Net Immigration	Total	
	(1)	(2)	(3)	(4)	(5)
1951-56	14.8	5.2	6.0	11.2	53.6
1956-61	13.4	8.7	4.1	12.8	32.0
1961-66	9.7	12.0	1.8	13.8	13.0
1966-71	7.8	12.0	4.3	16.3	26.4
1971-76	7.2	15.8	3.7	19.5	19.0
1976-78	2.1	5.3	1.3	6.6	20.4

(b) Age Distribution of the Population and Labor-Force-Participation Rates, 1951-78

| | Proportion of Total Population | | | | Labor-Force-Participation Rates | | | | | | | | | | | |
| | Under 15 Years | 65 and Over | Total (1)+(2) | 15-64 Years | Males [a] | | | | Females [a] | | | | Total [a] | | | |
	(1)	(2)	(3)	(4)	S (5)	M (6)	O (7)	T (8)	S (9)	M (10)	O (11)	T (12)	S (13)	M (14)	O (15)	T (16)
1951	30.3	7.8	38.1	61.9	n.a.	n.a.	n.a.	82.2	55.0	11.9	22.7	23.6	n.a.	n.a.	n.a.	53.1
1961	34.0	7.6	41.6	58.4	63.8	89.5	44.5	80.0	51.4	20.8	27.4	28.8	58.3	55.1	31.9	54.3
1971	29.6	8.1	37.7	62.3	57.8	87.1	49.1	76.1	48.3	33.0	28.3	36.5	53.6	60.0	33.1	56.1
1976	25.6	8.6	34.2	65.8	66.3	84.4	54.4	77.7	58.8	42.8	30.9	45.0	62.9	63.8	36.7	61.1
1977	25.0	8.9	33.9	66.1	67.1	84.0	56.0	77.7	59.0	44.2	32.3	46.0	63.5	64.1	38.3	61.5
1978	26.0	n.a.	n.a.	n.a.	67.9	84.0	58.4	77.9	60.5	46.3	33.4	47.8	64.6	65.2	39.8	62.6

(c) Hours of Work and Holidays, 1951-71

	Standard Work Week (hrs)		Mfg Employees Receiving 9 or More Days Paid Holidays (%)		Mfg Employees Receiving at Least Two Weeks Paid Vacation (%)	
	Office Workers (1)	Plant Workers (2)	Office Workers (3)	Plant Workers (4)	Office Workers (5)	Plant Workers (6)
1951	38.6	43.6	n.a.	n.a.	n.a.	n.a.
1961	37.7	41.3	29	19	82	23
1971	37.6	39.3	83	75	91	77

(d) Average Unemployment Rates, 1951-78[b]
(percentages)

1951-53	2.8
1954-57	4.3
1958-61	6.8
1962-70	4.6
1971-76	6.2
1977-78	8.1

n.a. = not available

[a]S = single, M = married, O = other, T = total.
[b]These periods are not based precisely on business-cycle peaks or troughs but are based on rough groupings of years with similar unemployment rates.

Sources: (a) F. T. Denton and Byron G. Spencer, "Does Canada Face a Labour Shortage in the 1980's?," Working Paper No. 76-12, Department of Economics, McMaster University, Hamilton, Ontario, October, 1976.
(b) Statistics Canada, *The Labour Force* (Ottawa, various issues), and *Historical Labour Force Statistics: Actual Data, Seasonal Factors, Seasonally Adjusted Data*, 1978 (Ottawa, 1979).
(c) Statistics Canada, *Perspective Canada II* (Ottawa, 1974), pp. 99-100 and sources cited therein.
(d) Department of Finance, *Economic Review* (Ottawa, various years); Bank of Canada, *Bank of Canada Statistical Summary* (Ottawa, various years).

The overall participation rates for men and women in 1978 were 78 percent and 48 percent, respectively, compared with about 82 percent and 24 percent in 1951. To put it another way, between 1951 and 1978, women moved from comprising only 22 percent of the labor force to comprising 38 percent.

The lower participation rates for men under 25 during the 1950s and 1960s were undoubtedly related to this group's desire to obtain additional education before entering the labor force. The reversal of this trend since 1971 suggests such influences as growing disillusionment with the net returns to extra schooling and/or, until recently, the desire to take advantage of Canada's liberalized unemployment insurance benefits.[3] Older men are apparently seeking retirement or are dropping out of the labor force because of difficulty in finding jobs or as their wives gain employment.

Women's expanded role in the work force may be the product of a variety of influences: the changing attitude of society toward their participation (or, should we say, a covert pressure on women to feel less than fulfilled unless they have a career apart from that of being a wife and mother), accompanied by a diminished desire for children; an increased desire by couples to acquire more material possessions in their search for happiness or to finance the spiraling costs of housing; the expansion in the number of service jobs suitable for women; and employers' desire to obtain the cheaper or part-time help that women are frequently ready to provide.[4] Generous unemployment insurance benefits after 1971 undoubtedly strengthened these forces, although the trend was already well-defined.

Another factor contributing to Canadian labor force growth has been increased net immigration since 1965,[5] accompanied by a decline in emigration to the United States to about one-third of what it was 15-20 years ago (apparently in part because of tighter U.S. immigration laws). Generally, about 50-55 percent of immigrants are labor force participants upon arrival. The net effects of migration on the labor force are shown in Table 2(a), column 3.

Offsetting, to a limited degree, the rise in the number of people in the labor force has been a drop in average hours worked per person per year since the 1920s, when the eight-hour day, 48-hour week began to be adopted. Following World War II, workweeks of 40 hours or less became common, and a gradual decline in hours has continued. Concurrently, the number of paid holidays and the length

---

[3] This latter phenomenon will be referred to again later on.

[4] See also Economic Council of Canada, *People and Jobs* (Ottawa, 1976), p. 72, and Gail C. A. Cook, ed., *Opportunity for Choice: A Goal for Women in Canada* (Ottawa: Statistics Canada in association with the C. D. Howe Research Institute, 1976), Chap. 4.

[5] In 1965-74, as in 1951-58, immigration averaged 170,000 people per year. In the intervening period it averaged only 94,000 people per year.

of vacation periods have been increasing. Numbers indicative of these trends are to be found in Table 2(c). In addition, the proportion of part-time workers has increased — for males, from 4 percent to 6 percent and, for females, from 22 percent to 25 percent between the early 1960s and the early 1970s.[6] Such changes have meant that, for 1961-71 and 1971-76, the number of hours worked expanded at a rate only one-half and two-thirds, respectively, that of growth in the number of workers.

These factors — the increase in the population of labor force age, higher participation rates among women, and expanded net immigration, offset to some degree by reduced hours of work per week, more paid holidays, and longer vacation periods — have been the main sources of the faster expansion of the labor force and hence of much of the sustained growth of national output over the past 10-15 years.

Four secondary influences of particular importance during the 1970s should also be discussed briefly before we finish this section.

• First, we have already suggested that the liberalization of unemployment insurance benefits in 1971 apparently contributed to the subsequent increase in the participation rates of various groups such as women and young people. Some elaboration of this point is probably useful.

Until more restrictive provisions were reinstituted in 1976 and 1978, the unemployment insurance program was at least as generous in Canada as in any other industrial country. A larger proportion of the labor force (99 percent) was covered than in other advanced nations; greater benefits were provided as a percentage of gross earnings (67 percent); and fewer weeks of employment were necessary (8) before benefits became payable.[7]

Early studies on the effects of the 1971 legislation focused on the increased unemployment that resulted from it. It was estimated that about one percentage point of the unemployment rate (that is, about 12-15 percent of total unemployment) was attributable to the inducement to labor force participation provided by the insurance program.[8] If only unemployment were increased, there would have

---

[6] Additional details of these trends can be found in Statistics Canada, *Perspective Canada II* (Ottawa, 1974), pp. 99-100, and in the sources cited therein; in Economic Council of Canada, *op. cit.,* Chap. 4; and in Paul Malles, "Canadian Labour Standards," in Economic Council of Canada, *Law, Agreement and Practice* (Ottawa, 1976).

[7] See Economic Council of Canada, *People and Jobs, op. cit.,* p. 272.

[8] Herb Grubel, Dennis Maki, and Shelley Sax, "Real and Insurance-Induced Unemployment in Canada," *Canadian Journal of Economics,* May, 1975, pp. 174-91; C. Green and J. M. Cousineau, *Unemployment in Canada: The Impact of Unemployment Insurance* (Ottawa: Economic Council of Canada, 1975); Fred Lazar, "The Impact of the 1971 Unemployment Insurance Revisions on Unemployment Rates: Another Look," *Canadian Journal of Economics* 11 (August, 1978): 559-69.

been no effect upon the level of actual output achieved in the economy. More recent work, however, which allows for the stimulative effect of government insurance payments upon consumption expenditures, and hence upon aggregate demand, indicates that, on the one hand, unemployment was actually *reduced* for males in the prime-age groups 25-44 and 45-64 without the participation rates' being significantly raised. Accordingly, national output was enlarged from this source. On the other hand, participation increased markedly for young men aged 14-19 and for women up to age 45 without their employment's being raised to any noteworthy degree.[9] The net effects, then, of the more liberal unemployment insurance benefits included both some expansion of output and an increase in the unemployment rate.

• Another secondary influence on output — and one with a clearly negative impact — has been the loss of man-days because of industrial disputes. This loss reached a peak of about 11-12 million man-days in both 1975 and 1976 — which, unless made up by overtime before or after disputes, would account for over one-half of one percent of total annual working time. The record for 1977 was much better, with days lost being noticeably less than in any year since 1971 and equaling only about one-tenth of one percent of total working time. In 1978 the losses rose again, to more than double their 1977 level.[10]

• Although frequently overlooked, a far more important source of reduced output than strikes (estimates place it at 11-25 times more important)[11] is time lost through sickness, or "days off" — that is, time away from the workplace quite apart from holidays, vacations, strikes, and official leaves of absence. Apparently, much of this lost time could be prevented if firms monitored the problem more carefully and developed programs to counter it. However, as yet relatively little has been done to deal with this type of output loss.

• Finally, deficiency of demand has, on occasion, reduced the rate of output growth. This was particularly true in the late 1950s, the very early 1960s, and the 1970s. For 1958-61 and 1971-76, unemployment averaged 6.8 percent and 6.2 percent, respectively (see

[9] Tom Siedule, Nicholas Skoulas, and Keith Newton, *The Impact of Economy-Wide Changes on the Labour Force: An Econometric Analysis* (Ottawa: Economic Council of Canada, 1976).

[10] See Labour Canada, *Strikes and Lockouts in Canada* (Ottawa, 1979), Table 1, and Clayton Sinclair, "Labour Is Angry," *Financial Times*, January 29, 1979.

[11] Richard Osler ("The 'Days Off' That Cost Firms Billions a Year," *Financial Post*, October 22, 1977) estimates that in 1976 this loss was eleven times greater than the loss owing to strikes. Clayton Sinclair ("Rising Absenteeism Costs Industry More Than Strikes," *Financial Times*, May 29, 1978) reports that in 1977 the loss was twenty-five times greater — equal to 4 percent of the total potential working time of the labor force. See also Jennifer Grass, "The High Cost of Absenteeism," *Financial Times*, September 25, 1978.

Table 2(d)). However, if one or more percentage points of unemployment in 1971-76 were attributable to the increase in labor force participation stimulated by the more liberal unemployment insurance benefits introduced in 1971, then one might argue that unemployment *per se* was not as serious a social problem in the latter period as in the former. This position is strengthened by noting that the proportion of those without work who were heads of families dropped from 46 percent in 1961 to 33 percent in 1974 and that the proportion of families where all members were unemployed decreased from 45 percent to 33 percent over the same period.[12] Again, requirements for reporting one's unemployed status were tightened in the 1971 legislation; this fact may also have contributed to the higher recorded unemployment rate in recent years.

During 1977-78, however, circumstances clearly worsened, for the average unemployment rate of 8.1 percent exceeded by at least one percent that for any year between 1958 and 1961 (although by the end of 1978, capacity utilization in manufacturing, at 89.2 percent, was above the average of the previous fifteen years). Moreover, the inducement to be on the unemployment rolls was lessened after the legislation was revised in 1976, so that one cannot attribute all of the increase in the unemployment rate to this cause. Forecasts for the domestic and world economies suggest that this problem will not be rectified easily or soon. We shall have more to say about current conditions — and future possibilities — later in this chapter and in subsequent chapters.

Labor Quality

Output growth is affected not only by the quantity of workers but also by the quality of their input. Some prefer to think of quality as a factor influencing the productivity of labor units. Others prefer to think of it as affecting the quantity of standardized units of labor being supplied. Either way, the quality of labor — which is a complex product of age, sex, education, experience, and hours of work — is a factor we must not omit when considering past and future output growth.

The reduction in hours of work per week in recent years may have resulted in greater productivity per hour — that is, output has possibly declined less than in proportion to the drop in hours worked. This may have been more important in earlier years, when working hours were much longer and the largest decreases in them occurred. However, as a proportion of the overall change in total output or in productivity per worker, the effect of this influence is undoubtedly quite small — and very difficult to measure.[13]

---

[12] Economic Council of Canada, *People and Jobs, op. cit.,* p. 210.
[13] For a useful discussion of this last point, see H. Lithwick, *Economic Growth in Canada,* 2nd ed. (Toronto: University of Toronto Press, 1970), pp. 10-11.

Some researchers have assumed that the quality of the labor force has been adversely affected by the increasing number of women entering the labor force; they base their assumption on the observation that women are paid less than men (about 30 percent less, on average, in recent years, even after adjustment for variations in education and occupation, with the difference being particularly marked for women over 25 and for those with less education).[14] Part of the discrepancy is apparently due to the fewer years of experience women have than men of the same age, owing to time taken off for their wifely and child-bearing responsibilities. The balance may be nothing more than discrimination against women, with no relation to quality of performance. Women, in turn, may have been willing to work for less, frequently on a part-time basis, just to supplement their husbands' incomes.[15] Again, methods normally used to estimate the effect of more women in the labor force — which do not take account of interaction effects among such factors as sex, age, education, and industry of employment — result in an overstatement of the reduction in labor quality resulting from their greater participation.[16]

The most important sources of labor quality changes have generally been thought to be those relating to improvements in the formal- and technical-education levels of the work force. Young people are typically much better educated than their parents, so that, as increasing numbers of them have entered the ranks of the employed, the average education levels of the labor force have been pushed up. Between 1960 and 1976, for example, the percentage of university graduates in the labor force more than doubled — from 4.5 to 9.5 — while the percentage with some post-secondary education rose from 8.5 to 32, with the proportions for men being modestly below, and those for women modestly above, the average.[17]

The marketplace recognizes to some extent the contribution that education and training make to workers' productivity: rates of return

---

[14]See Statistics Canada, *Earnings and Work Histories of the 1972 Canadian Labour Force* (Ottawa, 1976).

[15]For a detailed discussion of female earnings and other labor force characteristics of women, see Cook, *op. cit.*

[16]Peter Chinloy ("Source of Quality Change in Labour Input," Discussion Paper No. 77-17, Department of Economics, University of British Columbia, Vancouver, May, 1977, p. 19) says that "the results obtained [when allowing for interaction effects] indicate a negligible negative contribution [from more women in the labor force] even before adjustments for discrimination or imperfect information."

[17]The percentage increase is biased upward to some degree because the labor force surveys upon which it is based did not include all vocational training schools in 1960, whereas these schools were included in 1976. Still, since the bulk of these schools were established in the past fifteen years, the bias is not likely to be sufficient to invalidate the demonstration of growth in education and training suggested by the figures. (See W. D. Wood and Pradeep Kumar, eds., *The Current Industrial Relations Scene in Canada*, 1977 [Kingston, Ontario: Industrial Relations Centre, Queen's University, 1977], pp. 11-21 and 48.)

to increased education have been found to be fairly substantial, although they have declined somewhat in very recent years as more and more workers have acquired additional schooling.[18] It may be true, however, as some argue, that employers are increasingly demanding higher educational levels in new staff primarily as a means of screening applicants and not because jobs require additional education. To the extent that this is so, university graduates may get positions that high school graduates could readily handle, and the latter, in turn, may have to accept lower-paying ones.[19] Hence, to attempt to estimate precisely the contribution that extra education makes to productivity and economic growth by measures of differing returns to people with varying levels of schooling may not be entirely appropriate.

Offsetting to some degree the contribution that young people may make to output because of their superior education is their lack of experience and particular skills. The extent to which these influences counteract one another is difficult to determine with any degree of accuracy, although one recent study concludes that "the underlying contribution of education is reduced by one-half once adjustments are made for skill composition."[20] We do know, however, that, as young workers gain experience in their jobs, their monetary rewards are generally heightened — especially during the first 20-25 years of their working lives.[21] Thereafter, the market does not appear to reward additional experience very much. Other factors that may diminish productivity are associated with aging and may offset, or more than offset, any contribution to output that extra service yields.

Frequently, the presence or absence of education is particularly noticeable in the quality of management, for management affects the efficiency with which production and service are organized, the speed with which new technology is adopted and new markets are searched out, and the morale of the work force. The average educational level of managers has risen rapidly in Canada over the past fifteen years. Thirty-six percent of managers and non-government administrators had university degrees in 1971, compared with only 8 percent in 1961.[22]

Education is also a major contributor to differences in output per worker among the various regions of Canada — it is a far more important factor than the percentage of women working or the age of employees. A positive relationship exists between labor productivity

[18] See Economic Council of Canada, *Design for Decision-Making* (Ottawa, 1971), Chap. 9.

[19] See Lester Thurow, *Generating Inequality* (New York: Basic Books, 1975).

[20] See Chinloy, *op. cit.*, p. 19.

[21] See Economic Council of Canada, *Living Together: A Study of Regional Disparities* (Ottawa, 1977), pp. 70-71.

[22] Statistics Canada, *Census of Canada, 1961,* Series 3.1, *Labour Force* (Ottawa, 1962), and *Census of Canada, 1971,* Series 3.3-2, *Labour Force* (Ottawa, 1971).

TABLE 3

Employment, by Industry, 1946-76
(percentages)

Industry	1946	1961	1966	1971	1976
Goods:					
Agriculture	24.8	11.3	7.6	6.3	5.0
Fishing, trapping, and forestry	2.3	1.7	1.4	1.2	.9
Mines, quarries, and oil wells	1.5	1.3	1.7	1.6	1.5
Manufacturing	25.3	24.0	24.4	22.2	20.3
Construction	4.7	6.2	7.0	6.1	6.7
Utilities [a]	.7	1.2	1.1	1.1	1.2
	59.3	45.7	43.2	38.5	35.6
Services:					
Transportation, storage, and communications	7.2	8.1	7.6	7.6	7.5
Trade	12.0	16.9	16.5	16.5	17.3
Finance, insurance, and real estate	2.6	4.0	4.2	4.8	5.2
Community, business, and personal services	18.9	19.4	22.8	26.2	27.1
Public administration		5.9	5.7	6.4	7.2
	40.7	54.3	56.8	61.5	64.3
	100.0	100.0	100.0	100.0	100.0

[a] Statistics Canada now classifies utilities with the service sector. This would only accentuate the dominance of services.

Sources: Queen's University, Industrial Relations Centre, *The Current Industrial Relations Scene in Canada* (Kingston, Ontario, various years); Statistics Canada, *The Labour Force*, various issues.

in commodity production and the formal education level of the work force in the various provinces. To illustrate, British Columbia, Alberta, and Ontario — the three provinces with the highest productivity per worker — have the highest educational levels. In contrast, the four provinces with below-average educational levels — Newfoundland, Prince Edward Island, New Brunswick, and Quebec — also have below-average productivity levels in their goods-producing industries.[23]

These remarks lead us to consider, in a little more detail, interindustrial and related aspects of Canada's past and present economic development.

---

[23] Economic Council of Canada, *Living Together, op. cit.*, p. 39.

Changes in Industrial and Regional Economic Activity

Industrial Shifts

Some rather dramatic shifts in industrial employment have been occurring in Canada over the years. In the twenty years following World War II, the most important movement of workers was from agriculture (and, to a much lesser extent, from the other primary industries — fishing, trapping, and forestry) to other industries. Between 1946 and 1966 the proportion of total employment in agriculture declined from 25 percent to less than 8 percent. In the subsequent decade it declined more gradually to where it is now — 5 percent (see Table 3). Because output per worker was much higher in the sectors gaining workers than in agriculture (in 1961, for example, output per man-hour was nearly three times larger in the service industries than in agriculture), the average productivity of labor was raised by the shift.[24]

The process had other effects. For example, the population of Saskatchewan, the chief grain-growing province, declined — or at best just maintained itself — as workers moved to those provinces (British Columbia, Ontario, and Alberta) experiencing the most rapid expansion of industrial employment.

Concurrently, the average productivity of workers remaining in agriculture (who have had more capital and larger acreages to work with) increased rapidly from 1948 to 1973 — more rapidly, in fact, than productivity in any other sector except mining and utilities[25] — but is today still well below the level of productivity achieved in most other sectors.[26] However, since agriculture now accounts for such a small proportion of employment, any overall stimulative effect of additional fast productivity growth in this sector will be limited.

Other changes in productivity have come about because of variations in employment and in output growth within sectors. In the

---

[24]Statistics Canada, *Aggregate Productivity Measures, 1946-1974* (Ottawa, 1976), p. 22. Statistics Canada has also estimated that between 1961 and 1974 about 0.5 percentage points of the 4.1 percent annual growth rate of output per man-hour were a consequence of the movement of agricultural workers to commercial non-agricultural industries (see pp. 14-16).

[25]See Economic Council of Canada, *Eleventh Annual Review* (Ottawa, 1975), pp. 178-79. Recent work by P. Someshwar Rao (*An Econometric Analysis of Labour Productivity in Canadian Industries*, Discussion Paper No. 125 [Ottawa: Economic Council of Canada, 1978]) suggests that, in 1971-74, agricultural productivity growth was very low — only .06 percent annually. But Rao measures labor productivity by value added rather than by real domestic product, which is the measurement used in the *Annual Review*. The use of value added may not be appropriate (see J. D. May and M. Denny, "Post-War Productivity in Canadian Manufacturing," *Canadian Journal of Economics* 12 [February, 1979]: 29-41).

[26]In 1976, output per worker in agriculture was only 40 percent of that in commercial service industries and 34 percent of that in all non-agricultural goods-producing industries.

durables-manufacturing sector the faster advance of some industries with high output per worker (such as transport equipment and electrical goods) has helped, on occasion, to raise productivity. Sometimes, too, changes within sectors, such as in non-durables manufacturing, have reduced productivity growth slightly. The net effects on total manufacturing — at least for the 1961-74 period — have, however, been quite small.[27]

The predominant redistribution of employment in more recent years — although the trend started at least as far back as 1946 — has been the movement of workers from goods-producing industries in general to service industries, which now account for about two-thirds of all employment (see Table 3). The main goods-producing industry experiencing a relative — and, in 1977, an absolute — decline in employment has been manufacturing (although in 1978 the drop was reversed slightly). However, no rise in average productivity per worker has resulted from this shift, since output per worker is higher in manufacturing and other goods-producing industries than in commercial service industries.[28] Moreover, the service industry sector generally experiences lower rates of productivity growth than does the goods-producing sector.[29]

Regional Shifts

Another noteworthy trend of the 1970s is that population, employment, and industrial activity have tended to concentrate in British Columbia, Ontario, and Alberta, accompanied by some shift of manufacturing, construction, power generation, and mining from Quebec and Ontario to the two most western provinces, primarily because of Alberta's energy endowments (see Table 4). The three expanding provinces also have the highest per capita personal income and output levels. Particularly noteworthy is the change in Alberta's position with respect to individual personal income, which was only 98 percent of the national average in 1963 but rose to 104 percent in

---

[27] See Larry Blain, "Recent Developments in Aggregate Labour Productivity," *Bank of Canada Review,* January, 1977, pp. 11-13, and Rao, *op. cit.*

[28] This was not always so. In 1961, output per man-hour in service was about the same as that in manufacturing — $3.29 for the former versus $3.27 for the latter. In 1976 it was $4.87 versus $5.64. (See Statistics Canada, *Aggregate Productivity Measures, op. cit.,* Table 4.)

[29] For example, from 1966 to 1973, output per man-hour rose 1.1 percent annually in services and declined 0.1 percent annually in public administration, whereas for the total economy it increased 3.2 percent annually (Economic Council of Canada, *Twelfth Annual Review* [Ottawa, 1975], Table C-10). There are, of course, problems with measuring productivity in the service sector, especially in government administration, where no market value exists for output.

Note also that Rao's study, although questioned because of its use of value added for productivity estimates, finds that, even though there have been substantial differences in productivity growth among industries and shifts in the relative output shares of industries, the general effect of these developments on total labor productivity growth has been fairly inconsequential (Rao, *op. cit.*).

1977. (The decline in the average for the three Prairie provinces taken together between 1974 and 1977 was due primarily to lower agricultural output.) These regional shifts of activity to areas of higher output per person are raising average productivity growth, although the precise importance of these shifts is difficult to measure.

One other comment regarding changes in industrial structure is worth making at this point. Because of observations such as we have just made regarding how output per worker has been, and is, affected by interindustry shifts, it is sometimes believed that persistent differences in output and income per capita among the economic regions of Canada can be "explained" primarily by variations in the composition of industry in these regions. This is not so. Differences in output per worker *within* industries across regions (such as less lumber produced per worker in Newfoundland than in British Columbia) are far more important than industrial structure in accounting for variations in average labor productivity among regions (80 percent versus 20 percent).[30] In turn, regional variations in output per worker and in growth are a function of variations in labor quality (especially education) and, to a lesser extent, in capital stock per worker; the education and skill of management; the level and speed of adoption of new technology; and other factors such as scale of production,[31] transportation costs, resource endowments, and the urban environment.

Urbanization

In subsequent chapters we shall discuss in more detail a number of issues relating to increasing the capital stock per worker, the

---

[30]The exceptions are Saskatchewan and Prince Edward Island, where agriculture and, in the case of the latter, fishing — both low-productivity industries — predominated, and Quebec and Manitoba, where, because of heavy concentration in low-productivity industries — textiles, clothing, and food-processing — industrial structure was important (for more on the content of this and the following paragraph, see Economic Council of Canada, *Living Together, op. cit.,* Chaps. 5 and 7, and for the material upon which *Living Together* is based, see Ludwig Auer, *Regional Disparities of Productivity and Growth in Canada* [Ottawa: Economic Council of Canada, 1978]).

Another recent study (G. B. Norcliffe and B. Mitchell, "Structural Effects and Provincial Productivity Variations in Canadian Manufacturing Industries," *Canadian Journal of Economics* 10 [November, 1977]: 695-701) gives broadly similar results. It identifies a few other differences in productivity owing to industry mix, such as higher productivity in Newfoundland because of the pulp and paper, food, and chemical industries and in Saskatchewan and Alberta because of the petroleum-refining and chemical industries.

[31]The Norcliffe and Mitchell study (*op. cit.*) attempted to identify the effects of production scale on provincial productivity differences, but with the exception of Prince Edward Island and, to a lesser extent, Manitoba and Nova Scotia, these were quite unimportant. Even in these three provinces, residual factors — grouped under "output per worker differences" — were of much greater significance than scale in explaining variations in provincial manufacturing output from the Canadian average.

TABLE 4

Indicators of the Regional Distribution of Economic Activity, 1961-77
(percentages)

	Atlantic	Quebec	Ontario	Prairies	British Columbia	Canada[a]
	(1)	(2)	(3)	(4)	(5)	(6)
Population:						
1961	8.4	27.3	37.5	18.2	8.7	100.0
1971	9.5	27.9	35.7	16.4	10.1	100.0
1974	9.5	27.3	36.0	16.2	10.6	100.0
1977	9.5	27.0	35.9	16.6	10.7	100.0
Employment:						
1961	8.4	27.3	37.5	18.2	8.7	100.0
1971	7.6	27.2	38.1	16.6	10.5	100.0
1974	7.6	25.9	38.5	17.1	10.8	100.0
1977	7.5	25.6	38.5	17.5	10.9	100.0
Labor-force-participation rates:						
1961	48.1	52.8	56.7	55.6	51.8	54.1
1971	48.1	54.9	58.3	57.0	57.2	56.1
1974	53.4	58.0	63.4	62.6	60.3	60.5
1977	53.7	58.9	64.3	64.3	61.5	61.5
Regional shares of selected industries' value added:						
Manufacturing:						
1961	3.8	30.6	50.3	7.1	8.3	100.0
1974	4.2	26.7	52.9	7.2	9.0	100.0
1976	3.9	26.4	52.0	8.0	9.6	100.0
Construction:						
1961	7.7	23.7	33.2	24.2	11.1	100.0
1974	9.0	22.7	35.0	19.6	13.7	100.0
1976	8.1	22.9	30.7	24.8	13.4	100.0
Electric power:						
1961	7.0	28.8	37.1	15.1	11.6	100.0
1974	10.0	27.0	36.1	15.0	11.4	100.0
1976	10.5	30.5	31.2	15.4	12.0	100.0
Mining (including oil and gas):						
1961	2.7	14.8	31.6	41.4	5.2	100.0
1974	4.3	7.7	18.6	57.8	8.9	100.0
1976	4.8	7.2	12.8	65.0	8.9	100.0
Agriculture, forestry, fishing, and trapping:						
1961	7.3	16.3	27.7	34.2	14.3	100.0
1974	6.5	12.5	16.7	52.5	11.9	100.0
1976	7.0	12.1	20.6	46.4	14.0	100.0
Total industrial output:						
1961	5.2	26.1	42.0	16.8	9.7	100.0
1974	5.6	22.1	39.6	21.9	10.5	100.0
1976	5.5	21.8	38.3	23.4	10.9	100.0

Personal income per capita
(% of national average):

1961	68.9	90.1	118.4	89.9	114.9	100.0
1974	74.1	90.6	111.8	96.4	110.2	100.0
1977	74.6	93.2	109.3	98.4	110.3	100.0

[a] Owing to rounding or to the exclusion of the Yukon and the Northwest Territories, figures may not add to 100.0, particularly for population and mining.

Sources: For population and per capita income figures, see Statistics Canada, *National Income and Expenditure Accounts*, various years; for employment and labor-force-participation-rate figures, see Statistics Canada, *The Labour Force*, various issues, and *Historical Labour Force Statistics*, 1978; for value-added figures see Statistics Canada, *Survey of Production*, 1976 (Ottawa, 1977).

adoption of new technology, resource endowments, and economies of scale. However, the urban environment deserves brief mention here.

Urbanization has been an important phenomenon in Canada over the past several decades. By the 1970s, 70-75 percent of the population lived in centers of at least 5,000 people.[32] This trend is relevant to the discussion because income per person is positively related to urbanization and urban size. The higher per capita incomes in cities appear to be a result of higher participation rates in cities, an occupational structure in larger cities involving a higher proportion of senior managers, and economies of agglomeration owing to the availability of a variety of services needed in production. Once a city has about 1.5 million residents, however, the costs of congestion and similar problems apparently offset the advantages of size. Still, we should not overlook the contribution that urbanization has apparently made to income per capita growth (although it may contribute more diseconomies in the future as additional urban congestion arises).

Summary

Over the past decade or so not only has the labor force been increasing dramatically, but a fairly steady improvement in its quality has also occurred — primarily as a result of higher levels of education attained by the masses of young labor force entrants and those who have become managers. Quality may also have been improved somewhat by the increase in hourly input brought about by the reduction in hours of work. The lack of work experience of young people and new women workers countered, in part, the benefits of their stronger educational background, although exact estimates of this effect are difficult to obtain. Finally, the average productivity of

---

[32] This paragraph is based upon Economic Council of Canada, *Living Together, op. cit.*, Chap. 7.

the labor force has been enhanced by structural shifts in the economy — workers from low-productivity agricultural jobs moving to other industries, workers from less productive rural areas moving to urban areas, and workers from regions of low productivity moving to those of higher productivity.

Before considering other important factors affecting labor productivity, such as capital/labor ratios and technology, let us examine briefly the prospects for growth in the labor force, labor quality, and labor productivity from the sources of growth that we have already discussed in this chapter.

Future Labor Force Trends

Accurate predictions about the future of an economy are extremely difficult to make because so many social, economic, and technological variables may alter. This is true even when considering a single segment of the economy — the labor force. However, because several of the changes that have taken place in the labor force over the past decade or two have been so dramatic and will be impossible to duplicate in the next decade, we may be able to delineate some reasonable boundaries for future trends in the work force and its contribution to growth.

A number of things are clear:

• Birth rates have been declining fairly steadily since their peak in 1957. Hence, with the increases in the labor force resulting from the baby boom of the 1950s just about over, the expansion of the labor supply caused by more people reaching labor force age will taper off markedly in the 1980s. Even a new rise in birth rates in the near future would not affect the numbers available for the labor force until well into the 1990s — except in the negative sense of reducing the work force participation of women bearing children.

• We probably cannot expect substantial additional rises in the overall labor-force-participation rate of the sort witnessed in the past fifteen years or so. It is true that increases in the female participation rate in recent years have exceeded forecasts, so that the total participation rate is above earlier expectations.[33] But in comparing Canada with other advanced nations, we observe that its participation rate has risen to a point where, at 62.6 percent in 1978, it is greater than the 1977 U.S. rate of 62.3 percent and 1976 rates for Great Britain (61.6 percent), Japan (62.2 percent), and France and West Germany (about 55 percent each) and is only a little below the

---

[33]The Economic Council's CANDIDE projections to 1985 showed the overall labor-force-participation rate for 1978 as being 59.1 percent, whereas it was actually 62.6 percent (see T. Schweitzer, N. Mathieu, and J. Fortin, *Disaggregated Results of the Projections Presented in Chapter 5 of the Fourteenth Annual Review* [Ottawa: Economic Council of Canada, 1977], p. 12).

1976 rate for Sweden (64.8 percent). Moreover, the rates for Japan, France, and West Germany have actually declined over the past fifteen years, while Britain's has remained about the same.[34] Also, the 1976 and 1978 tightening up of requirements for unemployment insurance benefits may discourage any future rise in labor force participation that was stimulated by the more liberal benefits prevailing, for a time, after 1971.

• The average number of hours worked per year is likely to continue its decline as the workweek is further shortened, more paid holidays and lengthier vacations are introduced,[35] and more people from the recent labor force boom become eligible for longer vacation periods.

• The rules restricting immigration unless there are jobs available and no Canadians to fill them suggest that we are unlikely to see any swelling of net immigration flows offset the decline in potential labor force members stemming from the sources just mentioned.[36] In fact, the annual numbers of net immigrants entering the labor force in future may well be considerably less than the 60-65,000 of the past decade — usually the minimum numbers used in labor force projections.

• Although the absolute total, and the percentage, of working-time lost through strikes may, on average, be less in future than the high levels reached in 1975-76, there is little reason to expect any major long-run improvement in this aspect of labor force activity. (Perhaps a diminution in days taken off by employees, through better managerial control, or allowing workers to continue beyond the usual compulsory retirement age of 65 will be as important as anything in sustaining the contribution of labor to output growth.)

• A reduction in the unemployment rate to, say, a 4-5 percent range through an expansion of aggregate demand (as distinguished from a reduction owing to people dropping out of the labor force) would increase the growth of total output. But at best this would take a number of years to accomplish, so that any increments in output from this source are not likely to offset other forces making for a diminution in the rate of employment growth. Projections for the Canadian economy to the mid- or late 1980s do not provide any clear picture of what will happen to the unemployment rate. For

---

[34] Wood and Kumar, *op. cit.*, pp. 11-78.

[35] In 1969 only 1.5 percent of the labor force enjoyed six-week vacations. By 1976 this figure had increased to 18 percent.

[36] The results of recent econometric research indicating that additional immigration will quite conceivably raise the unemployment rate may also encourage authorities to be cautious in permitting any substantial rise in net immigration (see Gordon W. Davies, "Macroeconomic Effects of Immigration: Evidence from CANDIDE, TRACE and RDX2," *Canadian Public Policy* 3 [Summer, 1977]: 299-306, and Spencer Star, "In Search of a National Immigration Policy," *Canadian Public Policy* 1 [Summer, 1975]: 328-42).

example, estimates for 1979-86, inclusive, prepared for the *Fifteenth Annual Review* by the Economic Council of Canada under nine different possible sets of conditions relating to the state of domestic spending, exports, and federal monetary and fiscal policies suggested an average unemployment rate over these years of 8.6 percent. The situation was expected to deteriorate over this period as well, so that for 1986 the projected average unemployment rate for the nine alternatives was to be 9.6 percent.[37] Yet in the *Sixteenth Annual Review*, the Economic Council's projected average unemployment rate under five different conceivable sets of circumstances for 1980-85 was 5.7 percent, with *improvement* occurring over the years until the average of the five possibilities in 1985 was to be 4.6 percent.[38] Apparently the "discouraged worker" effect is now expected to be operative: as workers cannot find work, they leave the labor force and are then no longer counted as unemployed. The Ontario Economic Council and the federal Department of Industry, Trade and Commerce have provided other estimates which project unemployment rates between 1985 and 1990 of about 6 percent.[39]

In general, however, labor force and employment projections to the late 1980s anticipate that the rate of increase will taper off and become less than the very rapid growth of the past half-dozen years and also less than at any time in the past twenty-five years — about 2 percent annually at most, and probably less. In terms of absolute numbers, new workers added to the labor force in 1986-91 will about equal those added in 1956-61.[40]

What this growth pattern implies for future per capita income and welfare depends in part upon the dependency ratio — the ratio of total population to the labor force — and upon economic and social developments stemming from changes in the size or composition of this ratio. On the one hand, this ratio is expected to continue to decline modestly, or at least not to increase, for the next fifteen

---

[37] R. Preston, T. Schweitzer, and J. Fortin, *Fifteenth Annual Review: Statistical Documentation* (Ottawa: Economic Council of Canada, 1978).

[38] Economic Council of Canada, *Sixteenth Annual Review: Two Cheers for the Eighties* (Ottawa, 1979), p. 93.

[39] J. Sawyer, D. Dungan, and J. W. Winder, *The Ontario Economy: 1978-1987* (Toronto: Ontario Economic Council, 1978); Department of Industry, Trade and Commerce, Economic Analysis Branch, *A Structural Analysis of the Canadian Economy to 1990* (Ottawa, 1978). Perhaps the most important thing these various estimates tell us is that we should be cautious about forecasting future unemployment rates or relying heavily on any one set of forecasts.

[40] For example, see F. T. Denton and Byron G. Spencer, "Does Canada Face a Labour Shortage in the 1980's?," Working Paper No. 76-12, Department of Economics, McMaster University, Hamilton, Ontario, October, 1976; Economic Council of Canada, *Twelfth Annual Review, op. cit.*, Chap. 3; D. Foot *et al.*, *The Ontario Economy: 1977-1987* (Toronto: Ontario Economic Council, 1977), Chap. 2; and Department of Industry, Trade and Commerce, *op. cit.* This last study projects labor force growth at 1.83 percent annually for 1980-85 and at 1.27 percent annually for 1985-90. This is in contrast to the 3.3 percent annual growth experienced in 1965-70 and the 3.67 percent experienced in 1970-75.

years.[41] Hence, *ceteris paribus*, per capita incomes from this source will not be reduced and could be increased. On the other hand, the mix of dependents will alter, with older people becoming more predominant. This, in turn, may have a variety of effects. To illustrate, a larger proportion of society's resources will have to be spent on such items as health care, for older people have a hospitalization rate roughly three times greater than that of young people under 15.[42] Pension and other retirement fund payouts will increase, which may eventually create problems for provincial finances.[43] In general, though, we should not expect significant alterations in per capita income from changes in the size and composition of the dependency ratio through the 1980s.

Consider next the future *quality* of labor inputs. It would be overly optimistic to think that much, if any, additional improvement in the productiveness of an hour's work will come from further reductions in the workweek and in the number of working days a year. There are other possibilities: The proportion of potential labor force entrants with advanced levels of formal education will be increasing fairly steadily. In 1971-72 about 41 percent of potential new employees had some post-secondary school education. By 1984-85 about 59 percent of this group are expected to have post-secondary schooling.[44] However, as we have indicated, recent estimates suggest that the contribution of education *per se* has been overstated. To the extent, however, that these people have managerial and administrative training or can in any way enable others to benefit from their additional education, output should be enhanced. Also, as the large numbers of young employees and women who entered the labor force in the past decade gain on-the-job experience, their average output will expand. Yet, unless appropriate training programs are developed, their experience may not make them good substitutes for the loss of the skilled immigrants whom Canada has relied upon in the past to meet its needs.[45]

Migration of workers from rural to urban centers and from less productive to more productive regions may, as in the past, also be a positive force, however small, working to improve the quality of labor inputs and — depending upon how the measurements are taken — the average productivity of the workers concerned.

One major source of output growth in past decades, however, will not be duplicated in future. The improvement in the average productivity of labor as workers moved from the low-output-per-worker

[41] Denton and Spencer, *op. cit.*

[42] About 33 percent annually, versus 11 percent (see Statistics Canada, *Perspective Canada II*, *op. cit.*, p. 46).

[43] We shall return to this point in Chapter 4.

[44] Z. E. Zsigmond and E. Rechnitzer, *Projected Potential Labour Force Entrants from the Canadian Educational System: 1971 to 1985* (Ottawa: Statistics Canada, 1973), Table 9, pp. 34-35.

[45] We will refer to this topic again in Chapters 4 and 5.

agricultural and other primary industries (excluding mining) to the secondary and tertiary sectors cannot occur again. The proportion of the labor force in the primary sector — now about 6 percent — is not expected to diminish much further, if at all. Also, the shifts from manufacturing to the service sector that have been occurring, and may continue in the future,[46] are not likely to increase average output per worker very much, and certainly not as much as other sectoral shifts have done in the past. In fact, the service sector presently has a lower average output than does manufacturing.[47] Moreover, because manufacturing accounts for a smaller share of total employment now than in the past, the source of most productivity gain *within* sectors has been eroded. We probably should not expect any significant alteration in the traditional pattern of small productivity gains in the service sector, although the rapid adoption of inexpensive compact computors and revolutions in office data storage, data transmission, and communication may produce more pronounced productivity advances in services than we have become accustomed to expect.

To conclude this section, then, the growth in the labor force into the late 1980s will be much less rapid than it has been for the past two and one-half decades — perhaps 2 percent annually, or even less. Gains in output per worker will not be possible from additional structural shifts of employment from the primary sector to other sectors, and other intersectoral movements of personnel may contribute very little to increments in average output per worker. The future growth of education levels, the work experience of the labor force, and perhaps some improvement in labor force quality as it moves to more productive regional and urban areas will help to compensate for the lack of any major positive effect of additional shifts in industrial activity. However, broadly speaking, we can expect only a very modest net improvement in output per worker to result from the various influences discussed so far.

It would appear, therefore, that any future significant advance in average productivity must come about as a consequence of more capital per worker, rapid technological advance, new resource discoveries and techniques of extraction, greater economies of scale, and so on, if we are not to experience a much slower growth of total output and output per capita over the next 10-15 years. To these topics we now turn.

---

[46]This will depend upon a host of factors discussed in more detail in Chapter 4.

[47]The obvious question is, Why would workers move to services from manufacturing if, on average, output per worker were less in services? One explanation is that workers would be moving from those manufacturing industries — such as clothing — having below-average labor productivity to service sectors paying higher wages than in clothing, but less than the overall manufacturing average. Also, since wages are inflexible downward, relative wages among different sectors may adjust only slowly to changing job opportunities. In the meantime, workers may simply have to go where they can get a job, regardless of whether the pay is as good as where they were laid off.

3

Capital and Savings

Introduction

The contribution of capital to economic growth depends upon

- the rate of increase in the capital stock, which in turn depends upon incentives for additional investment and the supply of financing from domestic or foreign sources;

- the sectors in which capital is accumulated, whether the technology in these sectors requires a high ratio of capital to labor and capital to output, and whether this technology is changing;

- the efficiency of capital (and the technology it represents) in the use of natural resources, and changes in that efficiency;

- whether new investment embodies the most productive technology;

- the mix of structures, equipment, repairs, and inventories in each sector;

- the rapidity with which capital is "consumed" — that is, deteriorates or is made obsolete in the process of production.

The relative importance of each of these aspects of the role of capital is not easy to identify. In many instances we can do little more than indicate some of the trends that have occurred, and are occurring, and make some qualitative judgments about their significance. In so doing, our discussion should help to emphasize the many dimensions of capital's contribution to economic growth and the fact that the estimates we make of this contribution disregard many of these dimensions and therefore oversimplify the process by which growth is attained. In this chapter, in addition to looking at some of the trends in capital accumulation, we shall also review the sources of the savings so necessary for investment and economic growth, as well as some of the issues relating to the future supply of these savings.

Trends in the Growth of Capital Inputs

Aggregate Changes

Over the past one-half century, with the exception of the Great Depression in the 1930s, the net stock of physical capital in the economy has been expanding. Since World War II its annual compound rate of increase has been 5.6-5.8 percent, depending upon whether the entire period or the earliest to the latest peak years are used (see Table 5, column 1). The fastest growth rates occurred in the first 10-15 years following the war, with 1956-59 being an outstanding period in this respect. Since then the speed of accumulation has tapered off somewhat, but it is still much higher than for the 1929-45 period.

Physical capital has also been growing more rapidly than output over most of the past 30 years or so (see Table 5, column 5). The one exception is the prosperous period of the very early 1970s, when — although output was not even expanding as fast as for the previous 20 years — net new additions to capital stock did not keep pace. (We shall refer to this again later on.) Generally speaking, the trend has been toward a higher capital/output ratio for the economy.

Net capital stock has also been accumulating at a faster pace than employment growth, so that the ratio of capital to workers has been rising (see Table 5, column 2). This was particularly so in the 1950s, when the growth of capital stock was at its peak and the number of new workers was increasing more slowly than at any time in the postwar period. During the 1960s and, more particularly, in the 1969-74 period, when the labor force was increasing at a record rate, annual increments in capital stock per worker, although still positive, were the smallest of all the postwar years. By 1977, tangible capital per employed person was, on average, two and one-half times greater than in 1948 — $16,700 versus $6,700 (both figures in constant 1961 dollars).

Growth in the ratio of capital to workers is an important contribution to the long-run growth of labor productivity. Labor productivity in fact reflects increases in other inputs — including tangible capital — per unit of labor and in total factor productivity.

Sectoral Differences

There have been substantial variations in the rate of capital accumulation and in capital/labor ratios, and changes therein, in the different sectors of the economy. Some indicators of the changes that have taken place in these magnitudes over the past 25 years are

TABLE 5

Compound Annual Growth Rates of Net Capital Stock, Employment, and Output, 1929-77

Period	Net Capital Stock (constant $) (1)	Net Capital Stock per Employed Person (2)	People Employed (3)	Total Output (constant $) (4)	Capital Stock per Unit of Output (1) – (4) (5)
1929-45	1.0	.1	.9	3.5	-2.5
1929-39	0	-.6	.7	.5	-.5
1939-45	2.6	1.3	1.3	8.6	-6.0
1946-77	5.6	3.2	2.4	4.8	.8
Earliest to latest peak years in postwar period:					
1948-74	5.8	3.2	2.5	5.1	.7
Selected subperiods, peak year to peak year:					
1948-56	6.4	4.6	1.7	5.8	.6
1956-59	6.8	5.0	1.7	2.8	4.0
1959-69	5.4	2.4	2.9	5.2	.2
1969-74	5.1	1.6	3.4	5.3	-.2
Years since last major peak:					
1974-77	5.0	3.0	2.0	3.5	1.5

Sources: For capital stock figures see Statistics Canada, *Fixed Capital Flows and Stocks, 1926-1973 and 1973-1977* (Ottawa, 1974 and 1977); for employment and output figures see Statistics Canada, *National Income and Expenditure Accounts, 1926-1974 and 1963-1977*.

TABLE 6

Investment Growth Rates, Distribution of Capital Stock, and Capital/Labor and Capital/Output Ratios, by Industry,[a] 1951-77

Industry	Average Annual Year-over-Year Changes in Gross Investment Expenditures (current $) [a,b]							% of Total Capital Stock		Net Fixed Capital Stock (current $) ÷ Average Employment		Net Capital Stock ÷ Real Product, 1971
	1951-56 (1)	1956-59 (2)	1959-66 (3)	1966-69 (4)	1969-74 (5)	1974-77 (6)	1951-77 (7)	1951 (8)	1976 (9)	1961 (10)	1976 (11)	(12)
Goods:												
Agriculture and fishing	1.3	3.4	8.5	1.5	13.0	16.4	7.5	10.8	5.3	7,877	42,233	3.58
Forestry	10.3	-10.3	8.6	2.5	18.2	6.6	8.0	1.0	.7	3,992	24,820	1.63
Mining (including oil and gas)	20.8	1.2	16.4	10.5	12.6	24.0	14.3	2.6	7.3	32,049	179,751	3.71
Manufacturing	12.0	2.5	11.7	.8	12.3	11.0	9.5	18.6	16.6	8,763	28,286	1.50
Transportation equipment	-5.0	2.0	18.9	-5.7	11.0	9.6	7.3	1.2	1.2	–	–	1.06
Construction	24.0	-2.9	3.7	1.3	10.9	19.2	9.7	1.1	.9	1,951	4,481	.25
Utilities	9.2	12.4	6.9	7.6	12.0	22.9	10.9	9.3	13.9	123,683	468,796[c]	6.85
	10.3	3.0	10.0	3.5	12.0	16.7	9.7	43.4	44.7	11,021	47,036	2.24
Services:												
Transportation and storage	9.2	11.8	2.1	5.0	9.9	8.1	7.1	15.2	8.4	26,479	67,928[c]	2.28
Communications	14.0	11.4	7.6	9.6	13.9	14.9	11.5	3.3	5.4			2.37
Finance, insurance, and real estate	14.7	23.9	11.6	4.9	22.8	12.8	15.1	1.5	4.7	14,400	31,209	.61
Trade	7.7	3.8	2.0	11.6	11.1	9.4	7.0	5.1	4.1	3,840	8,296	.75
Commercial services	21.9	7.9	14.2	4.0	22.5	12.0	11.7	2.4	4.5			.72
Education, hospitals, and church institutions	11.7	7.7	11.6	8.4	-.8	7.5	8.2	5.8	9.2	5,890	17,682	1.27
Public administration	11.1	8.8	6.3	4.8	12.1	12.1	9.1	23.1	19.0			
Federal government	15.1	4.9	3.1	4.9	11.2	10.2	8.3	11.2	5.2	41,770	111,430	5.54
Provincial government	12.0	9.3	7.8	4.0	11.5	10.3	9.3	6.8	7.8			
Municipal government	8.4	13.3	7.5	6.0	13.8	15.6	10.3	5.1	6.1			

Total non-manufacturing											
9.4	9.4	6.3	5.9	11.6	11.0	8.8	56.4	55.3	9,339	33,568[d]	1.90
9.2	7.2	7.2	5.9	11.7	14.7	9.2	81.4	83.4	12,030	41,296	2.20
9.8	6.1	8.1	4.7	11.7	14.0	9.2	100.0	100.0	11,274	38,535	2.04

[a]The rates of gross investment are naturally affected by depreciation rates. Hence those industries that have a larger proportion of capital in buildings than in machinery and equipment will have lower depreciation rates, so that, for a given amount of gross investment, net capital stock would increase more. However, this possibility will not alter much the basic trends this table is designed to portray.

[b]Beginning and ending years were each weighted as one-half.

[c]Statistics Canada (*The Labour Force*, December, 1976) does not show the number of workers in utilities separate from those in transportation, communications, and storage, but the subdivision was available for 1975. By assuming that employment grew at equal rates in these two industries between 1975 and 1976, we are able to derive separate employment figures for each for 1976 and thus compute capital/labor ratios for that year.

[d]For 1976, because some of the service industries — for example, trade and community, business, and personal services — had a fairly large proportion of part-time workers, capital/labor ratios based strictly on total numbers employed may be biased downward. Hence, in making these calculations, I have assumed that two part-time workers are the equivalent of one full-time worker.

Sources: Columns 1-7: Statistics Canada, *Private and Public Investment in Canada: Outlook* (Ottawa, various years).
Columns 8-9: Statistics Canada, *Fixed Capital Flows and Stocks, 1926-1973* and *1972-1976* (Ottawa, 1976).
Columns 10-11: As for columns 8-9 for capital stock figures. Employment for 1961 was taken from the 1961 Census of Canada (Series 3) and for 1976 from Statistics Canada, *Historical Labour Force Statistics*.
Column 12: Statistics Canada, *Fixed Capital Flows and Stocks, 1926-1973* and *Real Domestic Product by Industry, 1971-1976* (Ottawa, 1977).

summarized in Table 6.[1] The table is largely self-explanatory, but a few points are worth highlighting.[2]

• Manufacturing's share of total capital stock has diminished slightly during the 25-year period under examination, apparently because of below-average annual growth in investment during three periods: 1956-59, 1966-69, and 1974-77.

• In each period, apart from the decline after the resource boom of the mid-1950s, mining has experienced more rapid annual increases in investment than the average for all goods industries. (Although not shown in the table, investment in the petroleum and natural gas industry has been the main source of investment strength in the mining sector over the past decade, with 17 percent and 30 percent average annual increases in gross investment outlays for 1969-74 and 1974-77, respectively.) As a consequence, this industry's share of total non-residential capital stock in the economy has nearly trebled (see columns 8 and 9).

• Although the service sector's share of capital stock is much the same now as in the early 1950s, annual increments of investment in several industries in this sector have been greater than average. This is particularly true for the prospering finance, insurance, and real estate industry; for communications (telephones and broadcasting); and for commercial services (the incipient practice of leasing as a way of obtaining capital equipment is reflected in recent numbers for this industry,[3] as are the large outlays for Montreal's Olympic facilities). Education and related institutions have also absorbed a larger share of total investment, although the expansion here has tapered off dramatically since the late 1960s, because by then the bulk of the stock necessary to cope with the rapid population growth had been put in place.

• The two periods after the cyclical peaks of 1956 and 1966 were quite similar to one another in terms of the very low annual rates of increase in investment occurring in the goods-producing industries, other than utilities and, in the second period, mining (see

---

[1] The distribution of gross investment (which has averaged 23-24 percent of GNE over the past twenty-five years) among government, business, residential housing, and value of physical changes in inventories is shown in Appendix Tables A.1 and A.2 in current and constant 1971 dollars, respectively.

[2] Note that columns 1-7 of Table 6 are not directly comparable to column 1 of Table 5. The former reflect average annual changes in *gross investment* from the previous year in *current* dollars and not, as in Table 5, the compound rate of increase in *net capital stock* in *constant* dollars. The stark difference in results is evident, for example, when comparing those for 1956-59. The average annual increase in net capital stock for these years was the highest of the years under review, whereas actual annual increases in gross investment (new capital, plus maintenance and repairs) from one year to the next were among the lowest in the postwar period.

[3] In 1976, outlays for equipment to be leased were up to about 7 percent of all business investment (Department of Finance, *Economic Review,* 1978 [Ottawa, 1978], p. 78).

columns 2 and 4). This is true both in current dollars and after adjusting for inflation (which was similar for business-capital formation in both periods). The 1966-69 period actually witnessed smaller percentage investment increases in manufacturing, and to a lesser extent in agriculture, than did the earlier period. If we compare the subsequent two sets of years (see columns 3 and 5), it appears from Table 6 that in 1969-74 the pace of investment increments was even stronger than in 1959-66 for all industries, including manufacturing and agriculture. However, once allowance is made for the faster rate of inflation in the later period, annual investment growth was generally lower then than in the earlier period. (This is true despite the fact that, even after adjusting for inflation, 1973 and 1974 were, following the worldwide boom of 1972-73, years of exceptional investment activity.)

• The well-known fact that there is high capital stock per worker in the utilities sector and, to a lesser extent, in mining and public administration is also evident (see column 11). These three sectors also have high capital/output ratios (see column 12). (Agriculture too has an above-average capital/labor ratio, although much less so than these other sectors.)

A final fact worth noting, not itself evident from Table 6, is that, although total manufacturing has a below-average capital/output ratio, some industries in this sector have substantially higher ratios: petroleum refining was 5.0 times the average in 1974, whereas paper products, chemicals, and primary metals were 2.9, 2.2, and 2.2 times the average, respectively.

Absolute numbers of capital/labor and capital/output ratios are perhaps not of much interest in themselves, but they are of considerable significance when we consider in which industries the future growth of the Canadian economy may tend to be concentrated and how much capital will be required per unit of output or per worker employed. To illustrate, energy-related investments — which are generally very capital-intensive — are becoming of expanding importance.[4] Their share in total new investment rose to 29.5 percent in 1976-77 from 20.9 percent in 1960-69 — primarily because of such installations as the James Bay hydro-electric project, the Syncrude oil sands development, and new nuclear power stations in Quebec and New Brunswick.[5] We shall have more to say later about such investment and its implications.

Differences have been occurring not only in total capital investment among sectors but also in the composition of the capital

---

[4] Such investments are classified in Table 6 under mining (coal mining, oil and gas wells, and oil sands plants); utilities (electric-power and gas distribution); transportation (pipelines); and manufacturing (the refining and processing of petroleum and natural gas).

[5] Department of Finance, *op. cit.*, p. 76.

going into these sectors. The past 25 years show a clear trend toward a greater emphasis upon machinery and equipment — at the expense of construction in manufacturing and institutions and of repair expenditures in utilities, government departments, and trade, finance, and commercial services (government businesses are included with the particular sector in which they operate — see Appendix Table A.3). This may have assisted in raising productivity, particularly in manufacturing, depending upon the technology represented by the change and the industries where the change occurred. But the lack of any decline in the importance of repairs relative to new machinery and equipment in manufacturing suggests that no general acceleration in the pace of adopting new technology has occurred in this sector and that, indeed, the tendency to repair existing equipment rather than replace it with new, more advanced installations may be a factor slowing productivity improvement. This possibility is in contrast to the situation in other sectors, where repairs are of diminishing relative significance.

There have also been shifts in the proportions of total investment going into government, business, housing, and inventories (see Appendix Tables A.1(b) and A.2(b)). In both current and constant dollars, the government sector's share of capital investment declined during the 1970s from its high of about 18 percent in the late 1950s and 1960s, so that once again it is back to 14 percent or so — not much higher than in the early 1950s. Housing has changed little over the decades, in constant dollars, but because of the more rapid price increases in this than in other types of investment, in current dollars it has been rising fairly steadily in importance since the early 1960s. In 1977-78 it was responsible for over 25 percent of all capital formation. Business fixed-capital formation in current dollars has not altered much from an average of about 58-59 percent, although in constant dollars its share for 1977-78 is a new average high of close to 63 percent of investment. Physical inventories perhaps register the most noteworthy change. For 1977-78 their proportion of total capital investment was down to about one percent in both current and constant dollars, an average approached only in the previous recessionary years of 1957-61. In other periods the annual share was over 3 percent, and often much higher.

Physical Capital and Productivity

Although a broad, positive relationship seems to exist between capital/labor ratios and output per employee among both industrial sectors and the major manufacturing industries[6] and although we

---

[6] For example, in 1976 the rank-correlation between capital/labor ratios and labor productivity for the sectors in Table 6 was about 0.7 percent, significant at the 2.5 percent level; within manufacturing the rank-correlation for both 1961 and 1974 was about .75 percent, also statistically significant (this latter calculation is based on Larry Blain, "Recent Developments in Aggregate Labour Productivity," *Bank of*

know, for example, that the grain farmer of today, working with his large tractor and complex supporting equipment, is far more productive than the pioneer of yesteryear, with his horses and simple machinery, changes in capital/labor ratios do not always produce straightforward, easily identifiable effects upon labor productivity. In the short run, cyclical forces are of overwhelming importance in explaining the quarterly variability in output per employee. Prior to at least the past two or three years, however, the degree of capacity utilization of capital and changes in this utilization "explain" over 99 percent of the variation. Now the suggestion is made that labor-hoarding by firms in recent years has been distorting the usual relationship between capacity utilization and productivity.[7] Even over the longer run it is not always easy to identify in aggregate, or over a cross-section of industrial sectors, any simple positive correlation between the growth rate of capital per worker and that of labor productivity,[8] although among manufacturing industries alone such a relationship does exist.[9]

These remarks intimate, therefore, that policies and circumstances that simply induce a higher capital intensity of production may, on occasion, raise labor productivity; however, in themselves they may not be a guaranteed "solution" to lagging productivity growth in the entire economy (and unless aggregate demand is sufficient, they may lead to greater unemployment). Cyclical factors tend to dominate in the short run, and over the longer run many other influences relating to the organization of production, the adoption of new technology, the ability and aggressiveness of management, and changing external competitive conditions are of

---

Canada Review, January, 1977, Table 4, p. 15). However, a rank-correlation between capital per worker and output per man-hour for the sectors in Table C-10 of the Economic Council of Canada's *Twelfth Annual Review* (Ottawa, 1975) reveals no statistically significant positive relationship.

[7] Blain, *op. cit.*, pp. 7-9.

[8] Blain found that, "at the broad economic level ... there was a positive, but not statistically significant, correlation between" the rate of change in the capital/employment ratio and output per worker (Blain, *op. cit.*, p. 12). See also W. D. Nordhaus, "The Recent Productivity Slowdown," *Brookings Papers on Economic Activity*, No. 3, 1972, p. 514, and L. Blain, "Secular Determinants of Productivity in Canadian Manufacturing Industries, 1961-1974," RM75-158, Bank of Canada, Ottawa, December 8, 1975, pp. 4-5.

Observe also — from Table 5, column 1, and Table 1, column 3 — that the years of fastest growth in net capital stock — 1956-59 — were also years of much-below-average growth in output per worker. In 1957-59, considerable idle capacity existed in the economy.

[9] Blain, "Recent Developments," *op. cit.*, pp. 13 and 15. P. Someshwar Rao (*An Econometric Analysis of Labour Productivity in Canadian Industries*, Discussion Paper No. 125 [Ottawa: Economic Council of Canada, 1978]) also notes that, in 1957-74, capital intensity contributed about 50 percent or more of productivity growth in non-durable manufacturing industries and in agriculture, finance, insurance and real estate, crude petroleum and gas, mining, and services.

considerable significance.[10] We shall examine some of these factors in subsequent chapters.

In the meantime, however, we will demonstrate, in a crude, aggregative way, the changing significance of these other factors, relative to labor and capital, as contributors to output growth. To do so, we depart briefly from what has been, up to now, our focus on labor productivity — or output per unit of labor — and examine growth from the broader view of "total factor productivity," involving inputs of labor, capital, and residual factors. This is a highly technical subject, involving a number of contentious issues. Sophisticated estimates have been made of the aggregate contributions of labor, capital, and residual factors to Canadian growth. Results differ somewhat, depending upon the time periods chosen, whether adjustments are made for the changing quality of capital, whether new technology is assumed to be incorporated into production via new capital or quite independent of it, whether durable consumer goods are counted as capital, and the like.[11] It is not our objective to provide any reconciliation of these results; we wish only to present some very rough estimates of the relative contributions of capital, labor, and residual factors during the major time periods we have been considering.

For this purpose we adopt a standard approach. It envisions the contribution of new technology as being separable from that of the additional capital employed. We assume that, over the long run, sufficient competition prevails that capital and labor receive just the value of their respective contributions to output. In this type of model the shares of capital and labor in national income will equal their marginal products. For the years 1951-77, capital received about 25 percent of national income, and labor, 75 percent.[12] When we know these shares and the growth rates of total output and of each factor input, we can determine the relative contribution of each factor and the residual to total output expansion.

---

[10]Some have argued that the consistency of any relationship between changing capital/labor ratios and productivity across industries also may be weakened because industries diverge in the extent to which anti-pollution equipment is necessary, although initial estimates do not suggest that this possibility is, as yet, all that important (see U.S. Department of Labor, *Monthly Labor Survey*, May, 1977 [Washington, D.C.: U.S. Government Printing Office, 1977], pp. 3-8).

[11]For a very brief survey of major studies carried out for the total Canadian economy over the years, see Appendix B.

[12]Statistics Canada (*National Income and Expenditure Accounts*, 3rd Quarter, 1976 [Ottawa, 1977], pp. xiv-xv) provides distributive shares for labor, property, and unincorporated businesses. One has to decide how to divide up unincorporated businesses into returns to capital and labor. Dorothy Walters (*Canadian Income Levels and Growth: An International Perspective* [Ottawa: Economic Council of Canada, 1968], pp. 193-99) concludes that labor's share of this total is about 60 percent. Based on this distribution, property income or capital income has averaged about 25 percent of total income over roughly the past twenty-five years.

TABLE 7

**Estimates of the Contribution of Labor and
Capital to Annual Growth Rates of Output, 1946-78**[a]
(percentages)

	Labor	Capital	Labor and Capital	Residual Factors	Total Output
	(1)	(2)	(3)	(4)	(5)
1946-77	1.8	1.4	3.2	1.6	4.8
	(37.5)	(29.2)	(66.7)	(33.3)	(100.0)
Earliest to latest peak years in postwar period:					
1948-74	1.9	1.5	3.3	1.8	5.1
	(37.3)	(29.4)	(64.7)	(35.3)	(100.0)
Selected subperiods, peak year to peak year:					
1948-56	1.3	1.6	2.9	2.9	5.8
	(22.4)	(27.6)	(50.0)	(50.0)	(100.0)
1956-59	1.3	1.7	3.0	-.2	2.8
	(46.4)	(60.7)	(107.1)	(-7.1)	(100.0)
1959-69	2.2	1.4	3.5	1.7	5.2
	(42.3)	(26.9)	(67.3)	(32.7)	(100.0)
1969-74	2.6	1.3	3.8	1.5	5.3
	(48.1)	(24.1)	(72.2)	(27.8)	(100.0)
1974-78	1.5	1.3	2.8	.8	3.5
	(42.9)	(35.7)	(78.6)	(21.4)	(100.0)

[a] Figures in parentheses are the percentages of total output growth accounted for by each of the influences distinguished.

Source: Growth rates for labor, capital, and output used in computing the above contributions are from Table 5.

The results are summarized in Table 7. Two things stand out: the greater relative importance of labor as a contributor to output growth since the mid- to late 1950s and the fairly steady decline in the comparative contribution of residual factors.

Capital's role has not altered in any consistent direction. Rather, the method of analysis used produces a greater contribution for capital in periods when, over the business cycle, it is not being nearly fully utilized and total output growth is slower. This result is particularly evident for the period from the cyclical peak at the end of 1956 to the next peak in 1959 and, although to a much lesser extent, in 1974-78. This effect also causes some reduction in the significance of the residual factors to our crude measure of total factor productivity. Apart from this influence, it appears true that a long-run decline in the residual has been occurring during the past 30 years. This diminution is consistent with our observation in the previous chapter that productivity-improving sectoral shifts, especially out of agriculture, have been less dramatic in the past decade or so. It also prods us to ask whether there are other aspects of the Canadian economy affecting its total performance that deserve close attention in this context now and in the future. Before considering some of these, we shall examine the sources of supply of capital for the Canadian economy and several issues relating to them.

The Supply of Savings

Increments to the capital stock require an adequate supply of funds and the foregoing of expenditure on current consumption — that is, savings. Where do these savings come from? What are the factors influencing the saving behavior of the various groups in our society? What are the implications of savings trends and the forces behind them for future supplies of funds and for the economy in general? These are the types of questions we address ourselves to in this section.

Domestic Sources of Funds

Government Savings

The various supplies of funds for investment are summarized in Table 8 for the years since 1950-51. Clearly, government contributions — in particular government net savings[13] — exhibit the greatest variability of any source of savings. Notice first the very low, or negative, net contributions during the periods 1957-61 and 1975-77. These were years when tight monetary policy was employed while, simultaneously, relatively large unemployment benefits and similar expenditures were being pumped into the economy to ease the burden on individuals out of work. Apart from these years the net contributions of government to total savings, although variable, have been fairly significant over the past quarter-century. The rise in personal incomes through increased output and inflation, as well as progressive tax rates on such incomes, has meant that tax revenues have risen more rapidly than GNP and that personal income taxes have been comprising a growing proportion of such revenues. In addition, government revenues have been augmented by Canada Pension Plan (CPP) and civil service pension contributions.

These forces in themselves might lead one to have expected that government savings would continue to be a steadily expanding share of total savings — as indeed seemed to be occurring throughout the

---

[13] Regarding the nature of capital consumption allowances by government, see note *b* to Table 8.

TABLE 8

Sources of Savings for Gross Capital Formation, 1950-77

(percentages)

	Government			Individuals and Unincorporated Businesses			Domestic-Owned Businesses and Govt. Enterprises			Non-Residents [c, d]					Residual Error of Estimate	Total Capital Formation		
	Net	CCA [a,b]	Gross	Net	CCA [a]	Gross	Net	CCA [a]	Gross	Retained Earnings	Net New Inflows	Total	CCA [a]	Gross		Net	CCA [a]	Gross
	(1)	(2)	(3)	(4)	(5)	(6)	(7)	(8)	(9)	(10)	(11)	(12)	(13)	(14)	(15)	(16)	(17)	(18)
1950-51	21.0	4.6	25.6	23.9	16.1	40.1	7.9	15.7	23.6	1.7	8.5	10.2	4.6	14.6	-4.0	58.9	41.1	100.0
1952-56	9.2	4.7	13.9	18.3	17.0	35.3	15.2	17.9	33.1	3.8	7.4	11.2	6.2	17.4	.4	54.2	45.8	100.0
1957-61	4.7	5.1	9.8	11.0	17.4	28.4	12.5	22.1	34.3	2.9	14.1	17.1	6.8	23.9	3.5	48.6	51.4	100.0
1962-66	10.6	5.7	16.3	15.7	16.1	31.8	12.9	21.5	34.5	3.5	6.5	10.0	7.2	17.1	.5	49.6	50.3	100.0
1967-71	15.3	6.2	21.5	15.8	15.4	31.1	12.4	19.4	31.8	4.5	.1	4.6	9.2	13.9	1.6	49.7	50.3	100.0
1972-76	8.2	6.0	14.2	26.4	13.5	39.9	9.3	16.3	25.6	5.8	5.3	11.1	9.1	20.2	.1	55.1	44.9	100.0
1975-76	.5	6.2	6.7	30.0	13.2	43.0	8.8	16.0	24.7	5.0	10.5	15.5	8.9	24.3	1.4	55.8	44.2	100.0
1977	-3.5	6.8	3.4	30.5	13.9	44.5	11.6	17.4	29.0	5.5	9.2	14.0	9.2	23.2	.1	52.6	47.4	100.0

[a] Capital consumption allowances — more commonly known as depreciation.

[b] Government capital consumption allowances are more in the nature of a bookkeeping entry rather than making available new funds for investment. The same amount is recorded each year under capital consumption allowances in GNP and as part of gross government investment in GNE. They are included, however, merely to show their relative importance in total gross savings.

[c] Statistics Canada has also made some estimates of the relative importance of foreign capital in gross fixed-capital formation, for the years 1946-70 (see *Canada's International Investment Position, 1968-1970* [Ottawa, 1975], p. 73), but they do not have the additional convenient subdivision between government and the private sector that Powrie's estimates have. Although the two sets of calculations differ by 1-2 percent on occasion, the fluctuations are very similar throughout the period common to both.

[d] These are probably minimum estimates of the role of foreign-controlled capital. They do not allow for foreigners' share of retained earnings and depreciation in portfolio equity investment in Canada (as distinguished from equity investment involving a controlling interest — that is, foreign *direct* investment). Also, in calculating *net* direct investment, the rate of return on investment by Canadian firms abroad was assumed to be equal to the rate earned on the capital of foreign-owned firms in Canada. If it should be less, then, for this reason too, net foreign investment may be understated.

Sources: T. L. Powrie, "The Contribution of Foreign Capital to Canadian Economic Growth," unpublished manuscript, 1977, and update for 1977, using his approach. For detailed annual information see Appendix Table A.4.

1960s. However, rapid urbanization, with its accompanying demands for more public capital and community services; the demands of society for more social services, such as health and education; the implications of fast technological change for greater government participation in smoothing out adjustment problems created thereby; the overlapping of the three levels of government and the rapid growth of their individual administrative and information-providing staffs; and pressure on government to expand programs in the direction of resolving regional and personal income inequalities have all greatly increased government outlays, especially at provincial and local levels, but also at the federal level with regard to transfer payments.

New spending proposals were not always scrutinized as carefully as they might have been as long as tax revenues were pouring in and funds were available from the CPP fund at interest rates below those the provinces would have had to pay on the open market. Once instituted, programs have been difficult to eliminate, even if no longer necessary, and often have not received the incisive reviews and assessments necessary to determine whether they should be terminated or revamped. Moreover, productivity improvements are difficult to attain in government administrative work or in associated government-financed programs, such as health and education.[14] Finally, on the one hand, the indexation of personal income taxes has reduced the gains in revenues the government might have received as a consequence of the inflation of incomes. On the other hand, the particularly high unemployment rates since the cyclical peak early in 1974 have led the federal government to inject spending of one form or another into the economy, while the simultaneously sluggish state of the economy has meant that tax revenues have not kept pace. It is therefore not surprising to see the relative size of net government savings diminishing in the 1970s.

Personal Savings

The single largest segment of total savings is supplied by individuals and unincorporated businesses. Of these, net personal savings have been increasing in relative significance in recent years. But this should probably not be construed as a long-term trend; it may be primarily a response to the higher rate of inflation over the past 10-15 years, as Chart 1 suggests.[15] Personal savings were also a larger-than-usual proportion of personal disposable income, and also

---

[14]These comments rely heavily on D. A. L. Auld, *Issues in Government Expenditure Growth* (Montreal: C. D. Howe Research Institute, 1976), especially pp. 54-56. This study also provides a good review of trends in government revenues and expenditures.

[15]For references and discussions supporting this position, see George M. von Furstenburg and Burton G. Malkiel, "The Government and Capital Formation: A Survey of Recent Issues," *Journal of Economic Literature* 15 (September, 1977): 840-42.

CHART 1

Personal Savings in Relation to Price Changes, 1947-77

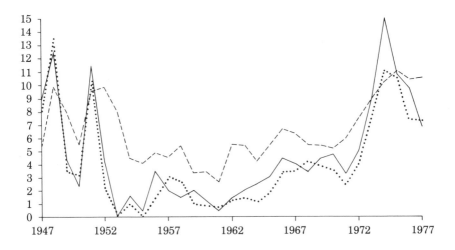

———— Implicit Gross National Product Price Index (annual percentage changes)
············ Implicit Consumer Price Index (annual percentage changes)
— — — — Savings As a Percentage of Personal Disposable Income

Source: Department of Finance, *Economic Review*, 1978 (Ottawa, 1978).

a more significant share of total savings, in 1948 and 1951 — both years of exceptionally high increases in price levels. Individuals save a greater proportion of their disposable income during inflationary periods, apparently in order to maintain some desired real rate of saving, to hedge against the uncertainty that inflation creates, or to compensate for the diminished capital value of existing fixed-price assets, such as bonds, savings accounts, and private retirement funds. The latter two possibilities seem to be more relevant in the recent period of fairly sustained inflation than in earlier single years of extreme inflation, since savings rates have not declined much with the easing of the rate of price increase in the past 2-3 years.[16] (The rate is still high by historical standards, however.)

The rise in multi-worker families may be contributing to greater savings rates. On the other hand, the higher participation rate of married women may be, in part, a response to inflation and the uncertainty it creates.

---

[16]Greater savings to buy housing — the price of which generally reflects the overall pattern of prices — may also be a small supporting factor in this last round of inflation. House prices normally do not decline much even after inflation subsides. If house buying were part of the initial motive for greater savings, such savings should remain at their new, higher rate in subsequent years.

The availability of many savings-incentive plans such as registered retirement savings plans and registered home ownership savings plans might have helped to stimulate more saving. But are these plans really a reason for greater saving, or are they simply a response by financial intermediaries such as banks, trust companies, and insurance firms to the higher savings rates — an attempt by them to attract funds from savers for purposes of lending to others? Certainly the real interest rates offered by the various plans are not higher than in earlier years after allowance is made for inflation. In fact, personal savings rates bear no clear relationship to interest rates.[17] Also, the commencement of the CPP, the growth of unfunded pension plans for government employees, and the presence of universal medicare programs and employer-employee benefit plans remove much of the stimulus for extra saving for old age or as a hedge against accident, sickness, and death.[18]

The indexing of personal income taxes is certainly not an explanatory factor in higher savings rates. At most, the indexing has abated, but not reversed, the tendency — evident since 1950-51 — for income taxes to take a progressively larger bite out of personal income and hence to reduce the portion of such income available for savings (and/or consumption).[19]

Personal savings do not appear to be a function of the changing age composition of the population or of changes in the average size of households. Competent econometric analysis has "failed to establish that there is any sensitivity of aggregate personal consumption and savings ratios"[20] to these variables.

In brief, then, the accelerated rates of inflation over the past several years appear to have been primarily responsible for the higher rate and larger share in total savings of personal savings, although other factors — such as more multi-worker families and the availability of savings opportunities — may have been contributing factors.

[17] See von Furstenburg and Malkiel, *op. cit.*, p. 840.

[18] Benefit costs for employees as a percentage of gross payroll have been increasing continuously — from 15 percent in 1953 to 31 percent in 1975 (see W. D. Wood and Pradeep Kumar, eds., *The Current Industrial Relations Scene in Canada,* 1977 [Kingston, Ontario: Industrial Relations Centre, Queen's University, 1977], pp. VI-86-87).

Note also that employer and employee payments into government pension funds and social insurance are treated as government revenues and not as part of personal savings.

[19] In 1950-51, personal direct taxes accounted for 7.0 percent of personal income. By 1970-71 they accounted for 17.5 percent, and by 1977-78, for 17.8 percent (Department of Finance, *Economic Review,* 1978 [Ottawa, 1978], pp. 135 and 182).

[20] F. T. Denton and Byron G. Spencer, "Does Canada Face a Labour Shortage in the 1980's?," Working Paper No. 76-12, Department of Economics, McMaster University, Hamilton, Ontario, October, 1976, p. 36. These authors' observation is based on their own work ("Household and Population Effects on Aggregate Consumption," *Review of Economics and Statistics,* February, 1976).

Domestic Corporate Business Savings

Gross savings of domestically controlled corporations have tended to decline in relative importance over the past decade (although some reversal of this decline is evident in 1977 and 1978), primarily because capital consumption allowances have become comparatively less significant and — particularly in the 1970s (except for the past year or so) — net savings (net profits after taxes and dividends) have also diminished.

Much of this diminution in domestic corporate savings, however, has been offset by increments in the savings of non-residents, including foreign-owned companies — which we shall comment upon more fully in the next section. Some would argue that, if accounting methods more appropriate to the times had been used, net savings would have dropped even more than the raw numbers suggest (although capital consumption allowances would be augmented proportionately). The view is that, under current inflationary circumstances, the use of accounting methods requiring depreciation allowances to be based on original purchase price rather than on current or estimated replacement cost and first-in-first-out (FIFO) inventory costing lower recorded expenses and thereby overstate profits.[21] While this is true for profits as reported by business, the numbers we use are from the national accounts, which subtract from profits an "inventory valuation adjustment" in arriving at net business savings. Hence a sizable portion of the impact of inflation upon net corporate savings has already been removed from our estimates.[22]

There are, however, two other reasons why net corporate savings may have been lower, on average, over the past few years, when both exceptional inflation and slow growth have co-existed. First, even without any net rise in corporate tax rates, taxes based on reported business profits before the inventory valuation adjustment made by Statistics Canada will represent a larger proportion of net profits after such adjustment than in the years before price rises became so significant. Only if inflation is brought under control, or bookkeeping to compensate for inflation is instituted, will this

---

[21] For a good discussion of these issues, see Richard Shaffner, "The Search for a More Reliable Measure of Profits," in Judith Maxwell, ed., *Policy Review and Outlook, 1975: Restructuring the Incentive System* (Montreal: C. D. Howe Research Institute, 1974), pp. 135-52.

[22] Clarence Barber has pointed out that, although corporate profits after tax as a percentage of national income appeared to rise above the average of the previous seven years in 1973-74, once adjustment was made by national statisticians for inventory valuation, undistributed corporate profits as a percentage of national income in 1973 equaled only their 1965-69 average — 4.7 percent — and in subsequent years were substantially below this average — 3.4-3.7 percent (see "Recent Canadian Economic Experience," speech delivered at the Practical Economics for Executives Conference, Gull Harbour, Manitoba, October 2, 1977).

difficulty be rectified.[23] Second, to the extent that profit rates are actually down somewhat — as they were at least until 1978-79, when they surged forward again in a number of industries such as pulp and paper, oils, department store retailing, base metals, and banks — the custom of firms to maintain dividend rates in such periods will reduce business retained earnings even more. This latter item is very much a cyclical phenomenon, however, and should not be important if prosperity returns.

Two other observations can be made about recent corporate financing. First, in the mid-1970s, firms were beginning to rely more upon borrowing or debt capital rather than upon equity capital for a larger proportion of their external financing — apparently because of the relative decline in the attractiveness of equities for private and professional investors.[24] Second, a long-run decline in the liquidity of corporations has been occurring, and greater reliance is having to be placed upon shorter-term (for example, bank and trust companies' loans) as opposed to longer-term borrowings.[25] We shall refer to these developments again later in this chapter, but first let us consider the final source of savings — non-residents.

Foreign Sources of Funds

Just as Canadian labor force growth has depended upon the increase in population from natural domestic sources and from net immigration, so the growth of capital stock has involved savings made available from both domestic and foreign sources. However, whereas relatively little doubt exists about the rough magnitude of the contribution of net immigration to labor supply,[26] the contribution of foreign-owned and -controlled savings to total savings has generally been largely understated.

This understatement has occurred because the retained earnings and capital consumption allowances of foreign-owned and -controlled firms have all too often been misleadingly counted as belonging to Canadians. This is unfortunate because these two sources of savings

---

[23] See Glenn V. Jenkins, *Inflation: Its Financial Impact on Business in Canada* (Ottawa: Economic Council of Canada, 1977). Note also that in 1973 some effective tax rate increases occurred in the minerals sector as profits rose, but more recently, decreases have been legislated for manufacturing and mining. It is therefore difficult to make any firm statement about whether average corporate taxation rates have altered much in recent years.

[24] See Donald G. Lawson, "Key Financial Problems: Changing Problems of Corporate Finance," paper presented to The Conference Board in Canada's Fourth Canadian Financial Conference, Montreal, June 28-29, 1977.

[25] *Ibid.*

[26] Perhaps this statement needs to be qualified somewhat. Precise figures are not easy to obtain because Canada, unfortunately, does not record emigration directly but computes it as a residual. Hence a fairly sizable margin of error can occur on occasion. (See B. W. Wilkinson, *Studies in the Economics of Education* [Ottawa: Queen's Printer, 1965].)

have never represented less than about 40 percent (as in 1957-61) of total foreign savings provided and on occasion (1967-71) have accounted for nearly 100 percent of them. Moreover, as a proportion of aggregate savings made available for investment in Canada, these categories together have increased quite steadily (at least until 1974, when they began to level off) and recently accounted for 14-15 percent of gross savings (see Table 8, columns 10 and 13).

The counting of the undistributed earnings of foreign corporations in Canada as Canadian savings has, in particular, led to gross underestimates of the role of foreign direct investment in net capital formation. Such earnings are a more important source of direct investment than are new inflows. Although it has been claimed, on occasion, that such investment in Canada is diminishing,[27] it has actually been expanding in dollar value and in 1972-75 increased more rapidly (10.6 percent annually) than in any year since 1957.[28] (The average annual increase in book value of foreign direct investment in Canada during 1957-72 was 7.4 percent.)[29]

The expansion of foreign direct investment has been coupled recently with debt borrowing abroad of unprecedented absolute magnitude, especially by the provinces and their crown corporations. Hence the relative importance of non-resident sources of gross funds for 1975-77 roughly equaled that in the previous peak years of capital inflows, 1957-61.

A range of factors influence the extent to which Canada relies upon foreign savings. With respect to debt capital, the breadth and depth of Canadian capital markets are frequently mentioned, but the traditionally higher long-term interest rates maintained in Canada than in the United States are generally recognized to be of prime importance. (It is of interest to note that, for the two periods when debt-capital inflows were relatively the largest — 1957-61 and 1975 to date — not only were restrictive monetary policies being followed in order to keep long-term interest rates well above U.S. rates, but Canadian unemployment rates were very high and net government savings were low.)

With respect to net foreign direct investment in Canada, the determinants of net inflows are more complicated. Manufacturing firms have often entered Canada to get behind the Canadian tariff or to follow competitors, while other firms have wanted to assure supplies of raw materials for themselves or to diversify their markets. When it comes to the sources of financing for these ventures, interest rate differentials have again been found to be important

---

[27] See Don McGillivray, "Interest Charges Taking Larger Payments Share," *Financial Times of Canada*, March 12, 1979, p. 6.

[28] Statistics Canada, *Daily Bulletin*, January 30, 1978, p. 5.

[29] Statistics Canada, *Canada's International Investment Position, 1968-1973* (Ottawa, 1977), p. 93.

explanatory forces for net inflows, as have such influences as the levels of profits in both Canada and the United States, firms' desire to diversify risk internationally, the perception of U.S. firms that the Canadian market is little more than an offshoot of their domestic operations and their financing expansion accordingly, and the extent to which Canadian government financial requirements crowd out domestic firms in absorbing increases in the money supply.[30] Once foreign firms are successfully established, however, their own profits and capital consumption allowances, not to mention the availability of financing from domestic financial intermediaries, provide a readily accessible source of many of the funds required to perpetuate their presence in Canada.

One thing is indisputable. It has been a policy of most Canadian federal and provincial governments to encourage continuous foreign capital inflows. We shall not attempt to discuss this policy in this chapter, but some of the issues relating to foreign borrowing, and especially to foreign direct investment, will be raised in subsequent chapters.

Summary

Government net savings have tended to vary directly with the level of national prosperity, while personal savings vary directly with the rate of inflation. In recent years of recession and inflation, therefore, the two types of savings have moved inversely to one another as proportions of national totals. Concomitantly, net and gross corporate savings of domestically owned enterprises have tended to decline somewhat in relative importance (although this trend may be reversing), whereas the comparable magnitudes for non-resident-owned corporations have tended to expand.

Future Trends and Issues with Regard to Capital

Discussion of the major issues with respect to prospective investment and capital requirements of the Canadian economy is best left for subsequent chapters. We need only say at this juncture that capital/labor and capital/output ratios are likely to continue their upward trend, so that, for a given desired increment in employment or output, the amount of new investment will increase. Moreover, the share of investment in GNE will have to expand as a greater demand for capital formation in the capital-intensive energy sector is experienced. In this section we confine ourselves to several remarks about capital supply.

First, the continuing serious worldwide economic problems, the limited possibilities for a quick turnaround in this situation, and the

---

[30]See also the discussion on foreign ownership in Chapter 6. For a review of the financial aspects of net foreign investment in Canada, see J. C. Pattison, *Financial Markets and Foreign Ownership* (Toronto: Ontario Economic Council, 1978).

accompanying heavy demands for government stimulative expenditures and welfare assistance suggest that minimal, if not negative, contributions to savings will tend to emanate from the government sector over the next decade at least.[31] Another feature of current government finance that will tend to produce this result is the fact that the CPP and many pension plans for workers employed directly (such as civil servants) or indirectly (such as schoolteachers) by various levels of government are not fully funded — that is, contributions required of workers over their laboring lifetime, plus any revenue earned by the fund on these contributions, will not be sufficient to provide the sums necessary to meet retirement benefits. Hence in the case of the CPP, for example, by 1990 — if not before — as more and more people become of pensionable age, additional taxes or other contributions to the CPP will be required to keep the fund solvent. Unless contribution rates are raised significantly, the CPP will be unable to provide funds for provincial governments, which have been borrowing from it at below-market interest rates. Furthermore, to the extent that these governments have not used the borrowed funds for productive investments yielding the revenues necessary to service and repay their debts, they will have to increase taxes or face larger deficits (and hence have negative savings) in order to meet their obligations.

Full funding of pension and retirement plans will, in turn, reduce personal disposable income. Some evidence exists that individuals may view such pension contributions as savings. If this is accurate, no decline in their consumption would necessarily occur and thus there may not be much, if any, increase in *total savings*. Expanded government revenues would replace diminished personal savings. Others, however, believe that full funding will enlarge the economy's total savings because individuals' consumption will be lowered somewhat, while government can concurrently invest the comparable amounts extracted from individuals.[32]

Personal savings, as a proportion of income, seem to have been primarily a positive function of the rate of inflation. Thus, if inflation were to be reduced over the coming few years, we should probably expect, *ceteris paribus*, that the relative contribution of household savings to the total supply of funds available for investment

---

[31] For empirical support of this observation see J. Sawyer, D. Dungan, and J. W. Winder, *The Ontario Economy: 1978-1987* (Toronto: Ontario Economic Council, 1978), pp. 38, 39, and 53; T. Schweitzer, N. Mathieu, and J. Fortin, *Disaggregated Results of the Projections Presented in Chapter 5 of the Fourteenth Annual Review* (Ottawa: Economic Council of Canada, 1977), pp. 2 and 7; and Economic Council of Canada, *Fifteenth Annual Review: A Time for Reason* (Ottawa, 1978), Table 9-2.

[32] These matters are reviewed in von Furstenburg and Malkiel, *op. cit.*, pp. 843-48. See also J. E. Pesando and S. A. Rea, Jr., *Public and Private Pensions in Canada: An Economic Analysis* (Toronto: Ontario Economic Council, 1977), and James E. Pesando and Lawrence B. Smith, *Government in Canadian Capital Markets: Selected Cases* (Montreal: C. D. Howe Research Institute, 1978).

would diminish somewhat.[33] And if, as has been true for some nations, the demonstration effect results in a decline in the propensity to save as more and more of the population becomes concentrated in large cities, then personal savings' share of total savings will drop further.[34]

These comments intimate that the decline in the relative contribution of *corporate savings* to total savings, about which some have expressed concern in recent times, may well be reversed. Of course, world and/or domestic recession may still make it difficult for corporations to achieve adequate profit rates to stimulate additional investment.

It is worth noting that concern has also been voiced about the decreasing corporate ratios of internal to external financing, of equity to debt capital, and of long-term to short-term indebtedness and about the negative effects these decreases may have on future investment in Canada.[35] Yet the definition of "acceptable" financial ratios seems to depend largely upon what a society has become accustomed to, upon its customs, and upon the institutional framework within which it operates. They are not absolutes. To illustrate, in Japan and, to a lesser extent, West Germany, undistributed corporate profits have frequently represented only 4-5 percent of total investment — a much lower percentage than in Canada. Even with internal depreciation included, Japan's corporate sector has commonly relied on external sources for over 75 percent of its financing. German business has been less reliant upon external sources; even so, over 45 percent of its funds have typically come from such sources.[36] Yet no other industrial country has consistently matched Japan in its pace of real economic expansion and in employment rates over the past two decades. Germany, too, is among the leaders in terms of its economic growth and prosperity. Even in Canada in 1950-51, business savings were a smaller proportion of total savings than during the 1970s (incidentally, 1951 was also a year of double-digit inflation); yet in those years, and the following half-dozen years, Canada, on average, enjoyed the most rapid growth of its history.

Again, Japanese — and, to a lesser degree, German — corporations have traditionally relied much more heavily on debt than equity capital and have still prospered.[37] Even among industries

[33] See Sawyer, Dungan, and Winder, *op. cit.*, and Schweitzer, Mathieu, and Fortin, *op. cit.*

[34] See Miyohei Shinohara, *Structural Changes in Japan's Economic Development* (Tokyo: Kinokuniya Bookstore, 1970), pp. 65-70.

[35] See Donald G. Lawson, "Key Financial Problems: Changing Patterns of Corporate Finance," paper presented to The Conference Board in Canada's Fourth Canadian Financial Conference, Montreal, June 28-29, 1977.

[36] Shinohara, *op. cit.*, p. 45.

[37] *Ibid.*

within Canada, wide divergencies exist with respect to the degree of reliance upon equity financing.[38]

Even the long-run decline in corporate liquidity and the growing reliance upon shorter-term borrowing (such as from chartered banks and trust companies) may not, in itself, be a cause for anxiety — although part of the trend is probably an outgrowth of the general uncertainty about the future state of business in Canada and, therefore, needs to be dealt with, insofar as possible, through improved domestic policies and cooperative international measures. The trend may partly reflect a gradual structural change in the economy as more and more individuals put their savings into claims on banks and other financial institutions, rather than directly into corporate stocks or bonds, and a shift toward more of a merchant-banking type of function for some financial intermediaries. Such developments may produce uncertainty and apprehension not because they are necessarily "bad business" or "bad economics" but simply because they represent change. As we adjust to them, they can become the norm to which we are accustomed.

The extent of the need to rely upon foreign sources of funds in the future is unclear. Projections of the balance of payments current-account deficit through 1985-86 vary widely, depending upon the assumptions made about domestic monetary and fiscal policies, the level of domestic investment, and exports. Using a simple average of nine different sets of assumptions, the Economic Council of Canada[39] estimates $9-10 billion a year. But such estimates — based upon existing balance of payments recording procedures, which exclude the retained earnings of foreign corporations in Canada — understate, even at current levels, the foreign contribution to *net* savings by about $3 billion and possibly more. And if the contribution to *gross* savings of depreciation and depletion allowances of such corporations were included, another $5 billion or so (at current levels) could be added to the figures. Hence, if these projections are accurate, annual dependence upon foreign financing could amount to about $18 billion in the mid-1980s.

Another set of estimates of the current-account deficit for 1985-86 has been made by the Ontario Economic Council.[40] These suggest

---

[38] See Canadian Imperial Bank of Commerce, "Selected Corporate Ratios, 1972-73," *Commercial Letter* 1 (February, 1977), which shows debt/equity ratios to be about 24 percent in mining and manufacturing; 65 percent in construction; 168 percent in transportation, communications, and utilities; 17 percent in wholesaling; 23 percent in retailing; and 64 percent in services.

[39] R. Preston, T. Schweitzer, and J. Fortin, *Fifteenth Annual Review: Statistical Documentation* (Ottawa: Economic Council of Canada, 1978).

[40] Sawyer, Dungan, and Winder, *op. cit.* See also the estimates of the Toronto-Dominion Bank (*Business and Economics* 8 [March, 1979], especially p. 12), which are somewhat lower than those reported in the text; this appears to be because they foresee higher aggregate domestic savings rates.

that it could amount to $12-15 billion. Consequently, Canada's annual dependence upon foreign sources of savings when retained earnings and depreciation allowances are included would be in the $20-25 billion range.

The magnitude of these numbers stimulates one to ask a variety of questions, such as, Will such amounts be available? Will the incentives be there to attract them? Is such dependence upon foreign funding really necessary? Is it desirable?

A full analysis of these issues would take us far beyond the scope of this monograph. But the discussion in subsequent chapters and appendixes, in focusing upon some of the structural and competitive problems of Canada's main commodity-producing sectors and the balance of payments, does suggest that they are valid questions and worthy of serious attention.

II

A SECTORAL VIEW

Introduction

By some measures it might be concluded that the Canadian economy has done quite well relative to the economies of other major nations of the Western world. Over the past decade Canada's rate of increase in employment has surpassed that of other developed countries; the average annual rate of real economic growth of 4.5 percent exceeded that of the United States (2.8 percent), West Germany (3.4 percent), France (3.9 percent), and Britain (2.1 percent); and the average yearly increment of 6.8 percent in the consumer price index was less than in Japan (9.1 percent), France (8.4 percent), and Britain (11.7 percent) and only a little higher than in the United States (6.4 percent).[1]

In terms of Canada's economic potential, one might argue that there also is much cause for optimism. Canada still has vast undeveloped energy resources and many other non-replenishable minerals; it has large forests, productive farmlands, and new opportunities in fisheries made possible by the adoption of the 200-mile limit. Its labor force is deemed to be quite well-educated by world and developed nations' standards. Transportation and communication systems are generally advanced technologically and functioning well — with the exception of bottlenecks of one sort or another in the export of grains. From this viewpoint one might conclude that, if Canada simply continues its traditional policies and practices, then in the absence of world economic collapse, nuclear war, or other occurrences of a similar catastrophic and far-reaching nature, its current economic difficulties will, in due course, work themselves out and a glorious new day of sustained prosperity and development will ensue — much like the period before the interruptions of the mid- to late 1970s.

This perspective may be too oversimplified to be realistic. It implicitly assumes that nothing of a fundamental and long-lasting nature has transpired in the world environment. But the world environment has, in fact, been altering. On the one hand, the developing

---

[1] These figures are found in Royal Bank of Canada, *Econoscope,* April, 1978.

nations, with the help of Western corporations and financing, have been more fully exploiting their resources of minerals and people; on the other hand, the pace of technological progress in certain of the larger industrial countries has been accelerating. The poor countries are demanding a larger share of the world's wealth — OPEC is an example of one method of trying to achieve this end — while the rich countries are becoming more protective and self-seeking in many ways (despite some liberalization of trade as a result of the Tokyo Round of GATT negotiations), and caught up in their own internal social and economic tensions. Real questions thus arise as to whether traditional policies and practices can produce the type of response necessary if Canada is to avoid being swamped by the events around it and as to whether following this strategy now will achieve anything more than simply to delay the time when massive, and economically painful, structural adjustments will be necessary in the Canadian economy.

The following three chapters review the changing Canadian situation from this perspective.

4

Manufacturing

Introduction

In the previous two chapters we examined broad developments with regard to labor and capital supplies. It is now appropriate to consider domestic and international developments with respect to the main commodity-producing sectors — manufacturing, mining, and agriculture — for these sectors are of crucial importance as generators of foreign exchange and in competing with foreign products. In this chapter we confine ourselves to manufacturing; in the next we highlight the resource industries.

The manufacturing sector lies at the heart of any industrial society. Without a substantial, advanced, diversified, and flexible processing sector, no nation can really claim to be industrialized in the sense of the word as we understand it. The day is perhaps coming when we shall speak realistically of some nations entering a postindustrial phase. The emphasis for such nations may be primarily upon the production and export of services and scientific and technical knowledge, along with basic outputs from their natural endowments of replaceable and non-replaceable resources. Even then, however, a strong manufacturing base will be essential if scientific knowledge is to be tested, applied, and related to efficient resource exploitation and the other practicalities of life. The processing sector may be as different from today's as today's is from that of the early nineteenth century, when spinning jennys and flying shuttles were the order of the day, and the pace of change will likely be even more accelerated than that of today. However, manufacturing of one form or another can be expected to remain an important component of every advanced nation's activity.

These observations suggest that we should not be in a hurry to dismiss the processing sector as irrelevant to the society of tomorrow but rather that we must make an effort to provide an environment in which it can prosper and, in prospering, adapt and adjust to a rapidly changing world.

We referred earlier to one or two developments in manufacturing. Our objective in this chapter is to examine in somewhat more depth a number of aspects and issues relating to the Canadian manufacturing sector — growth, composition, employment, productivity, competitiveness, technology, and foreign ownership — in the context of today's world.

The Record of Expansion

The 1961-74 period was one of substantial and sustained real growth in manufacturing. From 1961 until early 1966 the average annual rate of increase in manufacturing output was 8.4 percent. This rate declined somewhat over the ensuing five years to 4.2 percent, but picked up again to 7.9 percent from the end of 1970 until the beginning of 1974. Since that time, growth has been either negative, as in 1974-75, or at best about equal to that of the 1966-70 period.[1]

Over the 1961-74 period the number of jobs in manufacturing increased by 520,000, or 41 percent. The relative importance of the different major industry groups within manufacturing and the changes therein during this period are presented in Table 9. The sectors expanding more rapidly than the average for all manufacturing were rubber products (including plastics), machinery, electrical products, metal fabricating, transportation equipment, furniture and fixtures, and chemical products, in that order; with the exception of furniture and fixtures, all these sectors involved highly processed commodities and fairly sophisticated technology. Employment rose in all other industries as well, with the exception of leather goods (which experienced an absolute decline in employment), although less rapidly than the average for total manufacturing.

Unquestionably, the overvalued Canadian dollar of the late 1950s and the accompanying excess capacity of that recessionary period stimulated many cost-cutting measures in manufacturing, so that, when the Canadian dollar declined from above par with the U.S. dollar to be pegged in 1962 at U.S.$0.925, manufacturing was in a highly favorable position to take advantage of the opportunities this depreciation provided, both in replacing imports and in increasing exports, especially of finished products.

During the 1960s, highly manufactured products were the fastest-rising segment of Canadian exports. This expansion was led by the automotive sector, which accounted for about 22 percent of total shipments abroad in the early 1970s, compared to less than 2 percent at the beginning of the 1960s. The stimulus for this trade explosion was, of course, the auto pact of 1965, which provided for a rationalization of the Canadian automotive industry and its integration with U.S. production. Apart from automotive products, other

---

[1] Economic Council of Canada, *Fifteenth Annual Review: A Time for Reason* (Ottawa, 1978), Table 4-1, p. 52.

highly processed commodities — such as industrial machinery and equipment, communications installations, and defense-related equipment — were the fastest-growing segments of Canada's exports. (The Canada-U.S. Defense Production-Sharing Agreement, as well as improved export credit arrangements and trade promotion efforts, assisted this development.) Exports of these products (excluding automotive items) jumped from 10 percent of total sales abroad in 1960 to well over 15 percent by 1970. (Their share of total exports has not increased significantly since 1970, however, and on occasion has been less — as in 1974, when it was about 14 percent.)

Although world and Canadian tariffs were generally being reduced during this period (such reductions are normally made by discreetly lowering tariffs on imported inputs more than on the finished products), Canada continued to maintain fairly extensive tariff protection in a number of sectors (see Table 9, column 8). Moreover, a study of 82 manufacturing industries has shown that Canada actually *increased* its effective protection in 25 of them between 1961 and 1966. In at least 15 other industries, protection was reduced by no more than 2-2¹/₂ percentage points. In effect, in nearly half of Canada's manufacturing industries, protection remained virtually the same, or was increased, during these prosperous years. Between 1966 and 1970, although average effective tariffs on manufacturing were reduced from 20.1 percent to 16.9 percent on an unweighted basis (from 15.7 percent to 12.0 percent when weighted by value added in the individual industries), effective rates were raised modestly in 11 percent of the industries — such as slaughtering and meat processing; dairy products; wool, yarn, and cloth; some wood industries; paper boxes and bags; and glass and glass products. In another 26 percent of the industries, protection was lowered less than 2-2¹/₂ percentage points.[2] In addition, Canada maintained *de facto* import quotas on some labor-intensive products such as clothing. These were initially in the form of "export restraints" negotiated with developing countries. More recently, import quotas have been imposed on a fairly wide range of clothing and textile products from developing nations. Protection, then, has been a real part of the Canadian industrial scene as manufacturing growth has occurred.

Productivity and Competitiveness

Productivity growth in manufacturing has been strong over the entire postwar period. With the exception of 1960-65, when the annual growth rate of labor productivity was slightly higher in the United States than in Canada, the growth of output per unit of labor in manufacturing has, on average, been more rapid in Canada than

---

[2] B. W. Wilkinson and K. Norrie, *Effective Protection and the Return to Capital* (Ottawa: Economic Council of Canada, 1975).

TABLE 9

Selected Characteristics of the Twenty Manufacturing Divisions, 1961-74

| | Employment | | | | Wages and Salaries per Worker | 1974 (dollars) Net Capital Stock per Worker | Net Capital Stock per $ Shipments | Effective % Rates of Protection, 1966[a] |
| | 1961 | | 1974 | | | | | |
	% (1)	No. ('000) (2)	% (3)	No. ('000) (4)	(5)	(6)	(7)	(8)
Food and beverages [b]	14.9	188.9	12.4	220.9	9,048	23,345	.31	21.6
Tobacco products	.7	9.4	.5	9.6	10,260	19,167	.25	n.a.
Rubber industries	1.4	18.4	3.0	54.2	8,946	12,952	.31	24.6
Leather industries	2.5	31.4	1.5	26.4	6,716[c]	5,076	.21	35.0
Textile industries	4.9	62.5	4.2	75.6	7,795[c]	19,246	.55	26.1
Knitting mills	1.7	21.5	1.4	25.5	6,427[c]	7,176	.30	40.6
Clothing industries	6.9	87.7	5.7	101.7	6,241[c]	1,809	.08	26.4
Wood industries	6.3	80.0	6.0	106.6	9,738	17,946	.45	6.6
Furniture and fixtures	2.6	33.2	2.9	51.4	7,827[c]	5,467	.20	25.2
Paper and allied industries	7.5	94.9	7.4	131.3	11,621	51,318	.83	1.5
Printing and publishing	5.8	72.8	5.2	92.4	10,064	11,851	.41	7.4
Primary metals	6.9	87.2	6.8	122.2	11,912	46,031	.75	3.9
Metal fabricating	7.5	94.6	8.6	153.7	10,204	12,472	.30	16.8
Machinery industries	3.3	42.1	5.0	89.2	10,578	10,594	.25	2.7
Transport equipment	8.5	107.7	9.6	172.0	11,485	18,320	.22	-2.0
Electrical products	6.3	79.5	7.5	133.2	9,563	10,541	.26	17.7
Non-metallic mineral products	3.2	40.1	3.2	57.6	10,502	35,503	.81	11.5
Petroleum and coal	1.1	14.1	1.0	17.4	14,626	184,943	.60	60.4
Chemical industries	4.1	52.2	4.5	79.8	11,194	51,002	.73	12.9
Miscellaneous manufacturing	3.7	46.3	3.6	65.1	8,353[c]	9,539	.29	12.6
	100.0	1,264.9	100.0	1,786.0	9,830	22,970	.43	18.5[d]
								12.6[e]

[a] These represent the percentage decreases in value added that would occur in each industry if tariffs were removed on inputs and outputs, and no change in production methods occurred, after allowing for commodity taxes and adjusting protection downward for the proportion of the industry that is exported and must therefore face world competition without protection.

[b] Excluding alcohol.

[c] Industries where wages and salaries are far below the manufacturing average.

[d] A simple, unweighted average of individual industry rates.

[e] An average weighted by the value added of the individual industries.

Sources: Column 1: Statistics Canada, *General Review of the Manufacturing Industries of Canada, 1961* (Ottawa, 1965).

Columns 2-5: Statistics Canada, *Manufacturing Industries of Canada: National and Provincial Areas, 1974* (Ottawa, 1976).

Columns 6-7: Statistics Canada, *Manufacturing Industries of Canada and Fixed Capital Flows and Stocks, 1972-1976.*

Column 8: B. W. Wilkinson and K. Norrie, *Effective Protection and the Return to Capital* (Ottawa: Economic Council of Canada, 1975), Table 3-4.

TABLE 10

Average Annual Growth Rates of Output, Compensation, and Unit Labor Costs in Manufacturing, Canada and the United States, 1950-77
(percentages)

	Output per Hour		Hourly Compensation (U.S. $)		Unit Labor Costs (U.S. $)	
	Canada	United States	Canada	United States	Canada	United States
	(1)	(2)	(3)	(4)	(5)	(6)
1950-77	4.1	2.6	6.4	5.3	2.2	2.6
1960-65	4.5	4.8	3.6	3.5	-.9	-1.3
1965-70	4.5	1.4	7.5	6.0	2.9	4.6
1970-75	3.2	2.1	11.0	8.0	7.5	5.8
1976	4.6	4.3	14.0	8.3	9.0	3.9
1977	4.8	2.3	10.7	8.8	5.6	6.3

Source: U.S. Department of Labor, Bureau of Labor Statistics, Office of Productivity and Technology.

in the United States (see Table 10, columns 1 and 2). Although hourly wage rates have risen somewhat faster in Canada than in the United States, the better productivity performance in Canada meant that, until the 1970s, labor costs per unit of output increased more slowly there (see Table 10, columns 3-6). Canada was becoming more competitive in manufacturing vis-à-vis the trading partner with which it conducts 70 percent of its trade and to which over 80 percent of its highly manufactured goods are destined.

However, from 1970 to 1975, growth in output per hour, although still greater in Canada than in the United States, was not nearly high enough to offset the much larger hourly wage increases recorded in Canada. Hence, unit labor costs rose, at an average annual rate, by 1.7 percentage points more in Canada than in the United States (when expressed in U.S. currency). This outcome was partially the result of the rise in the Canadian dollar — after it was freed from its pegged rate of U.S.$0.925 at the end of May, 1970 — to about parity with the U.S. dollar.

In 1976, rapid wage increases, coupled with a dollar above par with the U.S. dollar until December, meant unit labor costs rose over twice as fast in Canada as in the United States, and Canadian competitiveness was further eroded with respect to that country.

During 1977 a drop in the Canadian rate of wage increases, plus the decline of the Canadian dollar, resulted in domestic unit labor costs' diminishing modestly in terms of U.S. dollars. Comparative numbers were not available, at the time of writing, on unit labor costs for 1978. Yet, with the Canadian dollar having declined another 9-10 cents from its 1977 average of U.S.$0.94 and with smaller wage increases in Canada than in the United States for the first part of the year, it appears that unit labor costs in Canada in relation to those in the United States have returned to approximately where they were in the mid-1960s. However, Canadian manufacturing was not fully competitive with U.S. manufacturing even in those years, so to be back in a similar position is in itself no cause for complete satisfaction — particularly in view of the changing world situation.

Before looking at the altering external environment and the associated domestic situation, some elaboration of the broad changes in Canada's cost position in manufacturing relative to the United States, using disaggregated data, is useful. The most recent authoritative study making such comparisons covers 1966-67 and 1974-76, and the results are presented in Table 11.

Notice, first, that in 1966-67, with few exceptions (the most significant being in wood products), Canadian labor earnings were higher, relative to U.S. earnings, than Canadian productivity, relative to U.S. productivity, warranted. The situation deteriorated in the 1970s; by 1974-75, labor earnings in Canada, compared with those in the United States, were about one-third greater than Canadian productivity, relative to U.S. productivity, would seem to justify. The situation was least favorable in non-durable goods. Productivity in Canada was about two-thirds of that in the United States, yet wages were 4 percent higher. With the exception of some types of paper products, the sectors represented there are also those for which Canadian tariff protection is the highest (see Table 9, column 8) and are sometimes supported by import quotas — as in the cases of textiles and clothing.

Canada's performance in the durable products represented in the sample was somewhat better than in non-durables, with productivity up to 94 percent of that in the United States. However, the particular product lines in this sample tend to suggest a more favorable situation for durables than may generally be valid. For example, transportation equipment, which accounts for nearly 40 percent of the value added of all the durables studied, is unusual because rationalization of the industry, and thus improved productivity, has occurred because of the auto pact. Again, the steel industry, comprising about 20 percent of the value added, is exceptional in Canada because of its technological forwardness and the aggressiveness of its management. Finally, the wood products sector — particularly sawmills and sash and door mills — benefits greatly from Canadian forest endowments. A more accurate representation of the situation for much durable products manufacturing in Canada may be that suggested by the miscellaneous category, which in the sample consisted of heating and air-conditioning equipment and major appliances. Here productivity in Canada relative to the United States is no better than that for non-durables.

TABLE 11

**Estimated Labor Earnings Differentials and Productivity Levels,
Canada/United States, 1966-76**[a]
(percentages)

	Can./U.S. Earnings, 1966[b]	Can./U.S. Productivity, 1967[c]	Can./U.S. Earnings, 1975-76[b]	Can./U.S. Productivity, 1974[c]
	(1)	(2)	(3)	(4)
Non-durable goods:				
Food processing	70	72	99	69
Textiles, clothing, and knitting	76	70	105	83
Paper products	85	76	109	77
Petroleum refining	82	37	101	70
Miscellaneous[c]	78	44	102	53
	77	53	104	68
Durable goods:				
Wood products	80	111	106	117
Metal products	82	70	105	93
Motor vehicles and parts	73	77	95	100
Miscellaneous	70	60	97	68
	78	73	101	94
Total sample	77	62	103	77

[a]Canadian-dollar basis.

[b]The Conference Board study recognizes that non-wage benefits were somewhat better in the United States than in Canada; but given that little change has occurred in the differences over the years studied, it was valid to compare the relative changes between the two countries. Some may argue that, because non-wage benefits are greater in the United States than in Canada, total Canadian wages are not really as high, compared with U.S. wages, as the figures suggest. However, to the extent that, over the period under review, paid holidays and vacation time in Canada have increased relative to those in the United States — as they seem to have done — average relative hourly wages in Canada would have increased more than the Conference Board estimates suggest.

[c]These calculations are based on values expressed in Canadian dollars only. The original source also has the results measured in terms of U.S. prices. The broad patterns are the same in terms of both sets of prices, although in terms of U.S. prices Canada's overall productivity performance is modestly better — 82 percent compared with 77 percent.

Sources: Columns 1 and 3: Adapted from James G. Frank, *Assessing Trends in Canada's Competitive Position: The Case of Canada and the United States* (Ottawa: The Conference Board in Canada, 1977), Table 4. However, to obtain the aggregate figures shown, earnings data for the more detailed industry data in the Conference Board study were weighted by 1967 and 1974 Canadian value added, respectively.
Columns 2 and 4: Table 9 of the above source.

The Conference Board report upon which Table 11 is based also makes a number of other observations of considerable relevance to our discussion:

• The rise in Canadian earnings to the point of being equal to, or even exceeding, earnings in the United States occurred in virtually all industries, not just manufacturing. Hence indirect, as well as direct, manufacturing labor costs in Canada drew much closer to those in the United States than they had been previously.

• The relative improvement in output per unit of labor input in Canada is partly a consequence of a greater application of capital per worker and not just due to greater labor efficiency *per se*. Even in 1967, machinery and equipment per employee in Canada was 1.4 times that in the United States. By 1974 this figure had risen to 1.6.[3] (The ratios would have been even greater if buildings had been included in the computation.) These numbers imply that capital is being used much less efficiently in Canada than in the United States. It thus appears that substantial scope remains for gains in the productivity of both labor and capital in Canada.

• Of the 33 industries studied in the sample, ten actually experienced relative productivity *declines* vis-à-vis the United States over the years under review. Four of these were in the food-processing sector,[4] four others were also non-durables,[5] and two were wood industries.[6] These declines occurred at the same time that Canadian wages were rising to equality or better with U.S. wages and capital/labor ratios were expanding faster in Canada.

This brief disaggregated look at the performance of Canadian manufacturing serves to emphasize the fact that Canadians had considerable success in raising wage and salary rates up to, or above, U.S. levels, even though manufacturing productivity growth did not warrant it. It was not surprising, therefore, that, commencing in late 1976, the Canadian dollar began to decline in terms of its U.S. counterpart. Only in this way could Canada's relative cost position vis-à-vis its dominant trading partner be restored, and this was accomplished fairly quickly, to the point of restoring the approximate position of the mid-1960s.

---

[3] The only two industrial groups for which productivity rose substantially while machinery and equipment per worker did not rise in Canada relative to the United States were transportation equipment and textiles, clothing, and knitting. The rationalization under the auto pact made possible the improvement in the transportation industry. In the other group, consolidation and mergers have been instrumental in improving efficiency without enlarging capital stock per worker. (See James G. Frank, *Assessing Trends in Canada's Competitive Position: The Case of Canada and the United States* [Ottawa: The Conference Board in Canada, 1977], pp. 112-13.)

[4] Slaughtering and meat processing, dairy products, fruit and vegetable processing, and breweries.

[5] Men's clothing, pulp and paper mills, paper bag and box manufacturing, and soap and cleaning products.

[6] Veneer and plywood mills.

The Changing International Situation in Relation to Canadian Development

Labor-Intensive Industry

As the foregoing developments were occurring in the domestic economy, the world economy was not standing still. The impoverished nations, struggling to achieve economic progress, were moving more and more into the production of labor-intensive commodities. They were establishing their own domestic plants and were making various concessions to attract large transnational firms to come and do the same. Concurrently, the transnational firms themselves were realizing that, in order to compete in the markets of the advanced world, they had to move many of their facilities for manufacturing low-skill-level, labor-intensive products to the developing countries to take advantage of their very low wage rates.

In this context it is worth taking another look at the record of manufacturing growth in Canada since the beginning of the 1960s. A number of industries — including textiles, knitting mills, clothing, furniture and fixtures, and miscellaneous manufacturing, to mention the most obvious ones — hired additional workers from 1961 to 1974. Employment in these industries increased by 95,000 over the period (see Table 9). Yet these are well-known to be labor-intensive industries, using large amounts of comparatively unskilled labor relative to capital and natural resources. The relatively low skill required of the labor input is reflected to a large degree in wages and salaries in these industries, which are much below average (see Table 9, column 5). The capital requirements per worker and per dollar of shipments for these industries, compared with the requirements for manufacturing as a whole, are also generally quite modest (columns 6 and 7).[7] Effective protection with respect to these industries averaged 26 percent (column 8).

Within these labor-intensive industries some subindustries and processes that depend upon a particular technology, domestic market orientation, or similar influences for their future may be able to become, and to remain, competitive in Canada without significant protection. Hence the removal of protection might not mean that jobs for all 350,000 workers involved — who account for 20 percent of manufacturing employment — would have to be found in other sectors of the economy.

On the other hand, subindustries and processes within many other sectors of manufacturing are also very labor-intensive and will come under increasing competitive pressures from low-wage developing countries. Hal Lary identified a wide range of products in these other sectors — printed material, several other paper products, wood

---

[7] The textile industry is an exception because, to permit mass-production techniques, it has become highly mechanized in recent years.

products, some rubber goods, electrical apparatus and appliances, basic machinery of a wide variety of classes, some canned foods, as well as certain non-metallic mineral products — as relatively labor-intensive.[8] We can observe from Table 9 (column 5) that food and beverages, the rubber industries, and — to a lesser extent — electrical products and the wood industries do indeed provide labor income per worker somewhat below the average for all manufacturing, which is indicative of the fact that some sections of these industries use substantial unskilled labor. Apart from the wood industries, effective protection for these industries is also high, averaging over 21 percent.

In addition, production involving standardized mass-production, assembly-line technology is also being shifted increasingly to developing countries by the multinational corporations, for many of the skills involved in such processing are very modest. C. P. Kindleberger's prediction of about two decades ago that automobiles would become the "textiles" of tomorrow is now being realized.

In brief, then, an assumption that only 20 percent of manufacturing employment (amounting to 4 percent of total employment in the economy) will be subject to more intense competitive pressures from the developing countries is very conservative. The figure could easily be closer to one-third of current manufacturing employment.

Over the longer term many of these industries will not be able to compete internationally with similar industries in the low-wage developing countries, even if all possible economies of scale are achieved, the best available production and managerial techniques are used, and the Canadian dollar remains about 15 percent (or even goes to 20-30 percent) below the U.S. dollar. Sustained high protection will be necessary if they are not to decline substantially.[9]

Technological Advance

At the other end of the spectrum are those products based upon new technological discoveries and applications.

There can be little doubt that the world rate of technological change has been accelerating, but Canada has been far from strong in its performance with respect to developing and applying new technology. Even in the early 1960s, total spending on research and development as a proportion of sales was less in Canadian industries than in nearly all U.S. industries.[10] Similarly, Canadian R & D as a

---

[8] Hal B. Lary, *Imports of Manufactures from Less Developed Countries* (New York: National Bureau of Economic Research, 1968), especially Table C-1.

[9] See Caroline Pestieau's studies of one segment of this labor-intensive sector (*The Canadian Textile Policy: A Sectoral Trade Adjustment Strategy?* [Montreal: C. D. Howe Research Institute, 1976] and *The Quebec Textile Industry in Canada,* Accent Québec series [Montreal: C. D. Howe Research Institute, 1978]).

[10] B. W. Wilkinson, *Canada's International Trade: An Analysis of Recent Trends and Patterns* (Montreal: Private Planning Association of Canada, 1968), Table 35.

percentage of GNP was less than for other major wealthy countries;[11] the proportion of domestic patents applied for by foreigners (95 percent) was much higher than for these same nations;[12] and when ranked by five different criteria of performance in technological innovation, Canada came tenth out of ten countries on three of them, and ninth and eighth on the other two.[13]

Canadian R & D outlays rose from less than one percent of GNP in the early 1960s to about 1.25 percent in the late 1960s. However, proportionately less R & D was done in industry, as opposed to government and universities, in Canada than in other developed nations. Government subsidies of various types did raise industrial R & D outlays by the amount of the subsidies, or more, and increased the number of patents obtained.[14] Still, overall research activity was small, with no growth in volume after 1969.[15] In 1975, R & D as a percentage of GNP was still lower in Canada than in any other developed nation for which data were available,[16] and by 1977 Canadian R & D outlays were down to .92 percent of GNP.[17]

The borrowing and/or adapting of technology from abroad is another method of moving forward with the pace of international technological advance. Here, too, Canada has done so with a substantial lag. On average, patents have been worked abroad four years before they are even granted in Canada,[18] and Canadian firms generally have been slower to adopt new machines and technological processes than have foreign operators.[19]

In the United States today, concerned voices are being raised regarding the longer-run implications of the transfer of front-line

---

[11]*Ibid.*, p. 121. The Canadian research effort totaled about one percent of GNP in 1963 as opposed to 3.1 percent for the United States and 2.2 percent, 1.3 percent, and 1.5 percent for the United Kingdom, West Germany, and France, respectively, in 1962.

[12]*Ibid.*, p. 123. In the United Kingdom and West Germany, the proportion was less than 50 percent, while in the Scandinavian countries it was about 70 percent. Belgium was closest to Canada, with 80-85 percent of its patents granted to foreign applicants.

[13]P. Bourgault, *Innovation and Structure of Canadian Industry*, Special Study No. 23 (Ottawa: Science Council of Canada, 1972), p. 38.

[14]D. G. McFetridge, *Government Support of Scientific Research and Development: An Economic Analysis* (Toronto: Ontario Economic Council, 1977), Chap. 3.

[15]Statistics Canada, *Research and Development Expenditure in Canada* (Ottawa, various years). For a useful short review see "Research and Development in Canada," *Bank of Montreal Business Review*, October, 1976.

[16]Organisation for Economic Co-operation and Development (OECD), *Science Resources Newsletter*, No. 2, Spring, 1977.

[17]Ministry for State and Technology, "Research and Development in Canada: A Discussion Paper," Ottawa, June 1, 1978, Table 5.

[18]O. J. Firestone, "Innovations and Economic Development: The Canadian Case," *Review of Income and Wealth* 18, No. 4 (December, 1972): 402. However, patents were sometimes worked in Canada before they were granted.

[19]D. Daly and S. Globerman, *Tariff and Science Policies: Applications of a Model of Nationalism* (Toronto: Ontario Economic Council, 1976), Chap. 5.

technology abroad by U.S. firms, especially when such transfers involve the training of foreign workers to the point where they can eventually replicate and improve upon the most current technology of the parent firm. This process implies the development of additional competition from such industrial nations as the members of the European Economic Community (EEC) and Japan, from the Communist countries, and from the rising OPEC nations and some of the more advanced developing nations. Increasing structural problems are foreseen in the United States, since workers may be displaced, not only from the more labor-intensive sectors employing fairly standardized technology but also from such technology-intensive industries as aircraft and chemicals. A weaker bargaining position in future trade negotiations with respect to supplying technology and related machinery, equipment, and specialist services is also expected to emerge as additional nations are able to bid on new contracts.[20]

If, indeed, these are valid concerns for the United States, how much more vulnerable is Canada's position with respect to international trade relating to new products and processes? In all but a relatively few sectors — such as nuclear energy, communications equipment, and specialized aircraft — in which particular product developments have occurred, Canada does not have front-line technology but rather is operating with relatively mature-product technology.

Measures to strengthen and encourage research and development in Canada were announced by the Canadian Minister of State for Science and Technology in June, 1978. This is not the place for a detailed assessment of these policies; it is sufficient to note that their implementation and the results therefrom will take time to occur. Moreover, continuity in the program is essential, for new products and processes will have to be continually forthcoming if trade flows are to benefit from such programs.[21] Also, adequate financial support from governments and/or financial institutions will be necessary to bring new ideas to the market once the basic research and design have been done. Because of the range of complex relationships between R & D and other aspects of the economy — such as skill levels, sufficient domestic financing, foreign ownership, and problems of achieving economies of scale — the desired results of a more technologically forward industrial economy and an improved

---

[20]See Jack Baranson, "A New Generation of Technology Exports," *Economic Impact* 19 (1977): 53-59.

[21]The "product cycle" — whereby new technological products are initially exported by the innovating country, then gradually produced by, and exported from, lower-labor-cost countries as the technology becomes more mature, standardized, and widely known — is today a recognized aspect of world trade flows. For an initial look at this theory, see R. Vernon, "International Investment and International Trade in the Product Cycle," *Quarterly Journal of Economics* 80 (May, 1966): 190-207.

international competitive position in high-technology products and processes is by no means assured by these measures.

Some of these relationships deserve to be mentioned at this point.

Skilled Personnel

It is often noted that Canada has a well-educated labor force. However, the absolute level of education achieved by workers is by no means the sole, or necessarily even the most important, attribute as far as technological advance is concerned. The educational and industrial mixes are also of vital significance. Scientific, technical, and engineering people are needed to digest, adapt, and apply the results of research elsewhere and to develop new products and processes. Skilled tradesmen are required to operate specialized tools and equipment. Progressive, flexible, and innovative managers and entrepreneurs are essential to mobilize and direct the contributions of the rest of the labor force and to bring to the marketplace, in an efficient manner, the results of scientific research.

It is not clear that the requisite workers will be in adequate supply in Canada when required. In the past Canada has, by and large, used immigration as a way of acquiring skilled tradesmen, rather than instituting adequate training and apprenticeship programs itself. The result is that today as many as three-quarters of the nation's supply of such personnel are foreign-born and -trained. This approach to building up the stock of this type of human capital has been cheap and easy in the past. Now, many of these tradesmen are in the upper age brackets and will be retiring. The choking-off of immigration means that replacements for them will be difficult to find.[22] New policies are being initiated to fill this gap, but these — like new programs for R & D — will require time to bear fruit.[23]

The low level of R & D in Canada in past years also means that the stock of scientific, technical, and engineering people with experience in this area is relatively small compared with that in other nations, as is the stock of such people in general in manufacturing. For example, the proportion of the manufacturing labor force in the professional and technical category in Canada was only 5.3 percent in 1971, whereas in the United States in 1970 it was 9.1 percent — over 70 percent higher.[24]

---

[22] Roderick Oram, "Time Runs Out on Replacement of Skilled Labour," *Financial Post,* February 18, 1978.

[23] Susan Goldberg, "Ontario Moves on Lack of Skilled Labor," *Financial Times,* June 12, 1978.

[24] John N. H. Britton and James M. Gilmour, *The Weakest Link: A Technological Perspective on Canadian Industrial Development,* Background Study No. 43 (Ottawa: Science Council of Canada, 1978), p. 75.

Similarly, there are questions to be asked about the adequacy of the numbers, education, and skill level of Canadian managerial talent in manufacturing.[25]

The relationship between characteristics of the labor force and a technologically progressive manufacturing sector is, of course, many-sided. To provide a supply of people with appropriate skills is, obviously, not enough; developing the industrial demand for them is also essential. Any new plans to strengthen the technological base of Canadian industry will need to come to grips with both these considerations.[26] This thought leads us to another dimension of the current Canadian manufacturing situation: the large presence of foreign-owned and -controlled firms.

Foreign Ownership

In 1974, foreign control was about 70 percent in electrical apparatus and machinery, 85 percent in chemicals, 96 percent in automobiles, 99 percent in rubber, and 100 percent in tobacco products.[27] The significance of foreign firms can also be seen by their prevalence among the *Financial Post*'s top 200 industrial corporations in Canada.[28] Of these 200 firms, 68 were 100 percent owned by foreign parent companies, 47 others were at least 50 percent foreign-owned, and another 20 had significant — and, not infrequently, controlling — foreign interests. In other words, roughly two-thirds of these firms were under foreign control.

A wide spectrum of opinion and empirical work exists on the implications of foreign participation in Canadian manufacturing. On the one hand, some claim that foreign firms bring with them, at below market price, the results of R & D from their home bases, as well as management expertise.[29] This position also may include the views that foreign firms exploit opportunities that would otherwise not have been exploited, thereby providing additional domestic employment, and that these firms' external ties provide ready-made marketing channels for exports. Again, advocates of foreign direct investment argue that value added per worker in foreign-owned establishments in Canada is, on average, higher than in

[25] Daly and Globerman, *op. cit.,* pp. 36-37.

[26] There is the old question of what is meant by a shortage. See, for example, the discussion of this issue in Milton Friedman and Simon Kuznets, *Income from Independent Professional Practice* (New York: National Bureau of Economic Research, 1945).

[27] Statistics Canada, *Daily Bulletin,* December 16, 1977.

[28] Industrial firms were defined as those for which over 50 percent of sales come from manufacturing or utilities.

[29] On this and other aspects of foreign ownership, see the views of Steven Globerman ("Canadian Science Policy and Technological Sovereignty," *Canadian Public Policy* 4 [Winter, 1978]: 34ff.).

domestically owned establishments and that, at worst, foreign-owned firms are no poorer performers than domestic firms in terms of R & D.[30]

On the other hand, others draw attention to the following facts:

- The importation of technical and managerial services from foreign parents is far from costless and is becoming one of the largest and most rapidly growing expenses for the Canadian economy.[31]

- A substantial proportion of the capital inflow is for the takeover of existing firms, not for establishing new plants.

- In a number of leading Canadian industries, foreign-owned establishments do not have higher value added per employee; in industries where they do, it is partially because they are usually larger than Canadian firms in the same industry — value added per worker generally increases with firm size — and partially because reporting methods bias the results in favor of foreign-owned establishments.[32]

- Foreign plants, like many Canadian plants, are geared to produce too many lines to achieve available economies of scale and have simply added to the fragmentation and inefficiency of manufacturing in Canada.

- Foreign-owned firms have, not infrequently, felt constrained with respect to the degree to which they could enter foreign markets with commodities produced with technology received from the parent or even developed in Canada[33] or, with regard to newly developed products, have found that manufacture for marketing has been moved to the home or some other country.[34]

- The technology obtained from abroad is often not up-to-date.

- Foreign-owned firms in Canada, in situations similar to those of Canadian firms with respect to sales, profits, depreciation allowances,

[30]D. Daly, "Economies of Scale and Canadian Manufacturing," unpublished manuscript, York University, Toronto, 1977.

[31]Statistics Canada, *The Canadian Balance of International Payments, 1973-1974* (Ottawa, 1977), Statement 19, pp. 70-71; M. J. Gordon *et al., A Study of Commercial Policy for Managerial and Professional Services* (Ottawa: Department of Industry, Trade and Commerce, 1976), p. 32. Gordon places the import value of technical, professional, and managerial services at nearly 25 percent of the total compensation to *all* Canadian personnel (including managers, engineers, and the like) in manufacturing and mining.

[32]To illustrate, value added for foreign subsidiaries in Canada includes services purchased from foreign parents, but the people providing these services from abroad are, of course, not counted. Hence value added *per employee* for foreign subsidiaries in Canada will be higher than for Canadian firms in which the employees providing similar services are included when the calculations are made. (Statistics Canada, *Domestic and Foreign Control of Manufacturing Establishments in Canada, 1969-1970* [Ottawa, 1976], pp. 11-15.)

[33]Ministry for State and Technology, *op. cit.,* p. 8; Arthur J. Cordell, *The Multinational Firm, Foreign Direct Investment, and Canadian Science Policy,* Special Study No. 22 (Ottawa: Science Council of Canada, 1971), p. 57.

[34]Cordell, *op. cit.*

government R & D incentive grants, and so on, spend less than half of what domestically owned firms spend on R & D,[35] yet they have been more disposed to apply for such subsidies and have enjoyed a higher probability of receiving them than have domestic firms.[36]

- A substantial amount of R & D by subsidiaries is nothing more than adapting products to local markets.[37]

- Canada's share of R & D outlays by U.S.-based transnationals is declining more rapidly than is its share of U.S. foreign direct investment[38] at the same time that the Canadian government has been providing 54 percent of total government-supported research grants received by U.S. firms abroad.[39]

- Foreign-owned firms do not have any better export record than do domestic firms; indeed, as they grow, they export more to affiliates and less to others, so that an ever larger proportion of Canadian exports are not arm's-length transactions.[40]

- Foreign-owned firms import larger proportions of their purchases than do domestic firms,[41] thus worsening Canada's current-account deficit while simultaneously reducing the market for domestic producers — with the result that achievable economies of scale within the Canadian economy are less than they otherwise might be — and quite possibly aggravating domestic unemployment problems.[42]

---

[35] McFetridge, *op. cit.*, p. 35.

[36] *Ibid.*

[37] *Ibid.*, Chap. 4.

[38] That is, as Canada's share of U.S. direct investment abroad fell from 27.9 percent in 1966 to 19 percent in 1972 — a drop of 32 percent — its share of R & D undertaken by U.S. transnationals abroad diminished from 22.3 percent to 14.3 percent — a drop of 36 percent (Daniel Creamer, *Overseas Research and Development by United States Multinationals, 1966-1975* [Ottawa: The Conference Board in Canada, 1976], p. 42).

[39] *Ibid.*, Table 5-5, p. 79.

[40] D. G. McFetridge and L. J. Weatherly, *Notes on the Economies of Large Firm Size,* Study No. 20 (Ottawa: Royal Commission on Corporate Concentration, 1977), pp. 85-91.

[41] See Wilkinson, *op. cit.*, pp. 145-52. Pierre Bourgault (*op. cit.*, pp. 88-91 and 106) reports that, on occasion, foreign subsidiaries in Canada may draw up engineering specifications that specify, or at least favor, foreign suppliers.

Note also that over time there does not appear to be any tendency for foreign-controlled manufacturing firms to increase the share of their purchases coming from domestic sources. Even excluding the automobile and parts sector, which dominates trade flows and shows a growing proportion of purchases coming from abroad because of the auto pact, the large foreign manufacturing firms in Canada imported 27 percent of their purchases in 1964 and were still doing so in 1971. (Department of Industry, Trade and Commerce, *Foreign-Owned Subsidiaries in Canada, 1964-1971* [Ottawa, 1974], Table 6, p. 14.)

[42] Britton and Gilmour, *op. cit.*, Chap. 5; Canadian Forum Limited, *A Citizen's Guide to the Gray Report* (Toronto: New Press, 1971), pp. 49-68.

• Foreign ownership and control frequently mean that decision-making on matters deeply affecting the Canadian economy takes place in head offices situated in other countries from a perspective not necessarily in keeping with Canadian objectives.[43]

These many facets of the influence of foreign direct investment on Canadian industry are not, in themselves, reasons to "blame" this foreign presence for some of the problems of Canadian manufacturing — even though the evidence seems fairly strong that foreign ownership and control have created more problems for the Canadian economy than they have solved. Rather, the pervasive presence of foreign direct investment gives one cause to be puzzled that so much macro-economic analysis and policy prescription have been forthcoming in Canada with little realistic recognition of the special circumstances and problems that this investment has produced.[44]

Economies of Scale

Perhaps the most important problem often associated with foreign direct investment in Canada is that related to the inefficient structure of Canadian industry. Compared with the huge markets of the United States, the EEC, and Japan, Canada's domestic market — although large in relation to the domestic markets of many nations in the world — is relatively small. The problem has been aggravated by foreign tariffs, which have limited access to foreign markets, and by domestic tariffs, which have induced foreign firms to set up assembly plants or more elaborate types of processing plants to serve domestic buyers from inside the country rather than export to them from abroad. As one or two foreign firms moved in, others followed in a bandwagon fashion so that they would not be at a disadvantage in supplying local needs. Concurrently, domestically owned firms were being established. The result has frequently been that none of these firms built plants large enough to be competitive in world markets; more important, even if the plants were seemingly of sufficient size, the plethora of lines produced — implying shorter runs, more retooling, and longer changeover times — resulted in higher unit costs than in foreign plants. Expansion to "world scale" was seldom undertaken, even as the domestic market expanded — apparently because both foreign and domestic firms feared starting a price war that they might not win or because they felt that others might do the same and hence they would all end up with much unused capacity. It is also commonly believed that the resulting fragmented industrial structure and relatively small market have discouraged

---

[43] Canadian Forum, op. cit., pp. 59-60.
[44] For an expansion of this view and a review of the economic literature in Canada to support it, see Stephen Clarkson, "The Two Solitudes: Foreign Investment Through the Prism of Canadian Economists," paper prepared for the Canadian Economics Association meetings, Fredericton, N.B., June, 1977.

domestic R & D and slowed the pace of diffusion of new technology from abroad.[45]

It would be imprudent, however, to place all blame for the inefficiency in Canadian manufacturing upon either the tariff structure or foreign — or domestic — firms. It is a historical fact that no contemporary industrialized nation, including the first ever to become industrialized — the United Kingdom — arrived at its current structure without having substantial tariff protection. An argument could be developed, therefore, that, given the Canadian tariff, domestic industrial and financial policies were sadly remiss in not taking proper advantage of the protection to ensure that an internationally viable industrial structure was being developed. It should be noted in this regard that knowledge of the cost-increasing effects of small-scale plants and low-volume production runs is not just now becoming apparent. It was mentioned in the Royal Commission on Canada's Economic Prospects in 1956 and 1957.[46] Twenty years earlier, in 1936, Marshall, Southard, and Taylor, in their study of foreign direct investment in Canada, observed that the smaller volume of output of U.S. subsidiaries in Canada was a major reason for their higher production costs in this country.[47] So ignorance that a problem was developing cannot be used as a rationale for the failure to come to grips with it.

Canadian policies have not consistently been designed to bring about an internationally competitive manufacturing sector. Apart from a few dissenting voices on occasion, any and all foreign capital has been heartily welcomed, and even induced, by competing intergovernmental grants, loans, guarantees, and assurances,[48] in order to create a few more jobs, regardless of whether the plants so attracted would be of efficient size and have sufficiently long runs to compete effectively with products from abroad either in the domestic market, with minimal protection, or in foreign markets. Not infrequently, provincial governments have required firms, either domestic or foreign-owned, to locate one of their plants within their

---

[45] Daly and Globerman, *op. cit.* For a detailed review of the literature on all aspects of the economies of scale, see D. J. Lecraw, *Economies of Scale in Canadian Manufacturing,* Study No. 29 (Ottawa: Royal Commission on Corporate Concentration, 1978).

[46] Royal Commission on Canada's Economic Prospects, *Secondary Manufacturing: Selected Industries* (Ottawa: Queen's Printer, 1956) and *Final Report* (Ottawa: Queen's Printer, 1957).

[47] Herbert Marshall, Frank Southard, Jr., and Kenneth W. Taylor, *Canadian-American Industry: A Study in International Investment,* Carleton Library Reprint Series No. 93 (Toronto: McClelland and Stewart, 1976), pp. 328-29.

[48] For a brief survey of current federal and provincial allurements to industry, see "Major Canadian Tax Incentives to Investment" and "Incentives to Industry," *Foreign Investment Review* 1 (Autumn, 1977): 14-15 and 22-24. In the foreword to that publication, then Minister of Finance Jean Chrétien made it very clear that he wished to remove the impression that the Foreign Investment Review Act is "designed, or is being applied, to 'block' foreign investment in Canada."

boundaries before they become eligible to bid on government contracts or purchases.[49] This narrow provincial protectionism has
added to the fragmentation of Canadian industry and has artificially
induced the growth of manufacturing in a way that may not be sus-
tainable in a competitive world.

Concluding Remarks

A variety of interrelated problems are confronting the Canadian
manufacturing sector at this time — the growth of facilities in developing countries for the production of labor-intensive and mass-
produced products at costs much below those with which Canadian
industry can compete, even with its dollar at a 15 percent discount
to U.S. currency; the rapid advance of new technology in other developed countries in contrast to the lack of a strong, up-to-date
R & D base over a broad spectrum of domestic manufacturing (which
is partly both a function of, and a contributor to, the dirth of scale
economies being achieved in production runs); the presence of many
foreign firms in almost every segment of manufacturing, contributing to its fragmented structure, as well as to the increase of imports
and the difficulties of establishing a stronger technological base
throughout the industry; a tariff structure and provincial protectionism that encourage the retention of inefficient-size production
units; and actual or possible "shortages" of personnel with the skills
to bring about the necessary improvements in production.

Other complications might have been mentioned, such as the
presence of many non-tariff barriers abroad that will probably continue to exist even as tariffs are reduced under the Tokyo Round[50]
and the pricing policies of the international shipping conferences,
which tend to be somewhat prejudiced against Canadian manufactured exports.[51]

However, even without going into additional details, the picture
is fairly clear. Canada's manufacturing sector is not in a strong position, not so much because its performance has deteriorated, but more
because the rapidly changing world situation has meant that what

---

[49] For a general discussion of the range of policies possible in instituting provincial
protectionism, see Carl S. Shoup, "Interregional Economic Barriers: The Canadian
Provinces," in Ontario Economic Council, *Issues and Alternatives, 1977: Intergovernmental Relations* (Toronto, 1977), pp. 81-100. For some details on Canadian
rules see M. J. Trebilcock, Gordon Kaiser, and J. R. S. Prichard, "Restrictions on
the Interprovincial Mobility of Resources: Goods, Capital and Labour," in Ontario
Economic Council, *op. cit.*, pp. 101-22, and A. E. Safarian, *Canadian Federalism and
Economic Integration* (Ottawa: Information Canada, 1974).

[50] About two-fifths of the American states have buy-at-home policies, and Japan,
through the use of marketing agencies and other devices, offers an inhospitable environment for competing products from other countries.

[51] See Ingrid A. Bryan, *Canadian Deep Sea Shipping Policy and the Merchant Marine
Issue*, Transportation Paper No. 3 (Toronto: University of Toronto/York University
Joint Program in Transportation, 1977).

TABLE 12

Unit Labor Costs in Manufacturing, Eleven Countries,
1972, 1973, and 1977[a]
(1967 = 100)

	1972	1973	1977
Canada	122.0	127.0	183.7
United States	118.1	123.2	168.3
United Kingdom	126.6	132.9	200.2
France	118.4	146.1	201.9
Denmark	117.3	147.6	210.8
Italy	152.2	172.5	233.9
Belgium	128.5	152.9	239.4
Sweden	132.8	148.5	258.5
Netherlands	139.2	174.0	272.1
Germany	164.3	211.7	293.4
Japan	159.7	195.2	326.5

[a] U.S.-dollar basis.

Source: Data obtained from the U.S. Department of Labor, Bureau of Labor Statistics, Office of Productivity and Technology, November 29, 1978.

may have been satisfactory in earlier years is no longer so. Maintaining the Canadian dollar at a 15 percent discount to the U.S. dollar, while useful in making Canadian products more competitive in domestic and world markets, is not likely, in itself, to be sufficient. Major structural changes in Canadian manufacturing operations are likely to become increasingly necessary.

A final illustration of this point may be useful. In Table 12, unit labor costs in Canada and in ten other developed nations are compared. Even in 1972 only France, Denmark, and the United States had lower unit labor costs, relative to 1967, than Canada. By 1973, with the decline of the U.S. dollar and the accompanying decline of the Canadian dollar, Canada's unit labor costs were relatively lower than those of all the other developed countries listed except the United States. By 1977, Canada's advantage appeared even greater. On this basis, one would have thought that Canada would have been gaining a progressively stronger position in its trade with all these nations other than the United States. Yet, as will be seen in Chapter 6, this did not occur. There is much more to competitiveness in world trade than relative changes in unit labor costs.

To conclude, we might ask whether there is a broader explanation of the difficulties Canada now faces — that is, a pervasive lack of vision, boldness, entrepreneurship, and aggressiveness in Canada, permeating both business and government.[52] Or perhaps we might

---

[52] See Wilkinson, *op. cit.,* pp. 152-55.

characterize the problem as Canada's propensity to look for the course of action that is easiest in the short run, regardless of adverse long-run implications. Welcoming foreign investment in the hope of obtaining short-run gains in job opportunities without any comprehensive industrial plan in mind is one manifestation of this proclivity. Another is importing technology — with a lag — rather than undertaking more domestic R & D. Provincial protectionism and an absence of adequate financial support for new ideas can also be interpreted from this perspective, as can Canada's depending upon immigration for skilled craftsmen rather than developing more of its own training programs. Whatever the reason, Canadian manufacturing is facing genuine problems that deserve careful attention. With these thoughts in mind, let us look briefly at the situation with respect to the other main commodity-producing sectors — mining, agriculture, and forestry.

5

Resource-Based Industries

Mining

A Brief Overview

Mining — including petroleum and natural gas but excluding processing — has regularly accounted for about $1^1/_2$ percent of total employment in the Canadian economy (although, during the great mineral boom of the mid-1950s, it employed slightly over 2 percent of the labor force).[1] However, the variety and abundance of Canada's mineral endowment and the enormous amounts of capital poured into this sector have resulted in output and export values of far greater significance than simple employment figures would suggest. The amount of net capital stock, in constant 1961 dollars, trebled between 1946 and 1956, rose two and one-half times more in the next decade, and then doubled between 1966 and 1976.[2] Net capital stock per worker, again in constant 1961 dollars, expanded from $10,346 to $77,812 — a sevenfold increase — over this period. It has risen faster than the capital stock in any other goods-producing industry and, indeed, faster than in most service industries, with the exception of the finance, insurance, and real estate sector.[3]

Productivity, measured as real domestic product per person employed, has increased more rapidly in this sector than in all other sectors, with the exception of utilities. From 1948 to 1970 the pace of productivity advance was nearly 5 percent annually, compared with 2.6 percent for the entire economy.[4] Much of this productivity growth is, of course, attributable to the enormous capital inputs. Total factor productivity, or the increase in output per unit of labor and capital combined, has actually been diminishing for metal mines since the beginning of the 1960s and for non-metallic mines since a peak in 1965.[5]

---

[1] Statistics Canada, *The Labour Force* (Ottawa, various issues).
[2] Statistics Canada, *Fixed Capital Flows and Stocks, 1926-1973* and *1972-1976* (Ottawa, 1974 and 1976).
[3] *Ibid.*
[4] Economic Council of Canada, *Eleventh Annual Review* (Ottawa, 1974), pp. 178-79.
[5] R. Elver, *Mineral Industry Trends and Economic Opportunities,* Mineral Bulletin MR 158 (Ottawa: Energy, Mines and Resources Canada, 1976), p. 24.

The changing relative importance of minerals, both crude and semi-processed, in Canada's export trade is evident from Table 13. Note especially the following:

• Mineral shipments abroad rose dramatically in relative importance between 1928-29 and 1955-56, from 11 percent to nearly 30 percent of total merchandise exports. Much of this expansion occurred because of the post-World War II resource boom in Canada, when foreign capital — particularly from the United States — helped to develop these resources.

• Mineral exports, especially of petroleum and natural gas, continued to gain in relative importance from the 1950s to the 1970s, so that — even with the huge stimulus to trade from the auto pact — they remained at roughly 30 percent of total merchandise sales abroad. (It has also been established that even Canada's secondary manufactured exports depend indirectly upon the nation's non-replenishable resources.)[6]

• Crude mineral exports (excluding petroleum and natural gas) have risen more rapidly than have exports of semi-fabricated minerals.

Surprisingly, considering that Canada sees itself as having become progressively more industrialized, a larger proportion of its minerals are shipped abroad in crude forms today than in 1928-29. Canada is more like a developing nation than an advanced industrial nation in the sense that developing nations also export about one-half of their minerals in crude forms.[7] But in contrast to what is occurring in developing nations — which, over the past decade, have reduced the share of crude minerals (excluding oil and gas) in their total mineral exports (from over 52 percent to less than 50 percent) — crude minerals have become a larger percentage of total Canadian mineral shipments abroad (rising from 49 percent to 53 percent). Moreover, Western developed countries (the United States, Japan, and those of the EEC) have generally been increasing the share of their total mineral imports in semi-processed rather than in crude forms; but in their trade with Canada, only the United States has been moving in this direction and even then at a slower pace than with respect to its imports from all other nations taken as a group. Another way of expressing the growing significance of crude minerals is to note that these exports account for two to three times as large a share of Canada's GNP today as they did in the late 1920s. Only in the iron and steel sector — which, interestingly

[6] Harry H. Postner, *Factor Content of Canadian International Trade: An Input-Output Analysis* (Ottawa: Economic Council of Canada, 1975). See also J. R. Williams, *Resources, Tariffs and Trade: Ontario's Stake* (Toronto: University of Toronto Press for the Ontario Economic Council, 1976).

[7] For this observation and the rest of the paragraph, see B. Wilkinson, *Minerals in Canada's International Trade*, Centre for Resource Studies Working Paper No. 2 (Kingston, Ontario: Queen's University, 1978).

TABLE 13

Canadian Merchandise Exports, by Selected Major Commodity Division, 1928-78

	Million Dollars				Percentages			
	1928-29 (1)	1955-56 (2)	1964-65 (3)	1977-78 (4)	1928-29 (5)	1955-56 (6)	1964-65 (7)	1977-78 (8)
Crude minerals (except oil and gas)	55	555	1,113	4,735	4.4	12.2	13.4	9.9
Semi-processed minerals	84	711	1,185	4,754	6.7	15.7	14.3	10.0
Petroleum and natural gas	2	70	372	4,484	.1	1.5	4.5	9.4
	140	1,336	2,670	13,973	11.2	29.4	32.2	29.3
Automobiles and parts	42	51	279	11,287	3.3	1.1	3.3	23.7
All other	1,064	3,149	5,361	22,334	85.3	69.4	64.7	47.0
	1,246	4,536	8,310	47,594	100.0	100.0	100.0	100.0

Sources: Statistics Canada, *Trade of Canada* and *Exports by Commodities* (Ottawa, various issues).

enough, is the sole mineral-processing sector almost entirely Canadian-owned — have fabricated exports been expanding more rapidly than exports of crude ores and concentrates.

The expansion of mineral exports over the past twenty years or so reflects a number of important internal developments: the opening up of the vast Quebec-Labrador iron ore deposits during the 1950s (for export primarily to the United States), the exploitation of Saskatchewan's potash reserves from the early 1960s onward (also primarily for U.S. markets), the growth of coal and copper ore (especially for sale to Japan) and zinc production (for Japan and the EEC), and the development of oil and natural gas for both domestic needs and for export to the United States.

Foreign direct investment has generally been important — and frequently been dominant — in these ventures and resulting trade flows. About 58 percent of metal-mining assets and 68 percent of petroleum and natural gas extraction are foreign-controlled. At least 60 percent of foreign subsidiaries' exports are to parents or affiliates, and these firms also purchase about 75-80 percent of their total imports from parents or affiliates.[8]

Canada's mineral production and reserves in relation to the world as a whole and to non-Communist countries, and its share of U.S. imports, are shown in Table 14. For eight of these leading minerals — asbestos, tungsten, zinc, uranium, iron ore, nickel, silver, and molybdenum — and perhaps strontium, Canada has at least one-sixth of known economically recoverable reserves in the non-Communist world. It has a particularly strong position with respect to asbestos (60 percent), tungsten (40 percent), and zinc (31 percent). In 1974-75, Canada was the world's largest producer of asbestos, zinc, nickel, and strontium and the second-largest producer of molybdenum, silver, selenium, colombrium, uranium, and potash. Its relative importance as a producer of nickel and asbestos has been declining, however.[9] Its reserves and production of conventional petroleum are relatively small. However, when oil sands are introduced, Canada's position is enhanced considerably. Synthetic crude reserves, recoverable by existing surface-mining techniques, add another 27 billion barrels to Canada's existing 6-8 billion barrels. If known *in situ* methods of extracting synthetic crude from depths

[8] Statistics Canada, *Corporations and Labour Unions Returns Act — Part I — Corporations,* 1975 (Ottawa, 1978), pp. 128-29. The percentages reflect the share of total assets held by corporations at least 50 percent owned by foreigners. For the oil industry the percentages would now be lower, since both Husky Oil and Pacific Petroleum have been taken over by Canadian firms. See also Department of Industry, Trade and Commerce, *Foreign-Owned Subsidiaries in Canada, 1964-1971* (Ottawa, 1974).

[9] In 1950, Canada produced 80 percent of the world's nickel and 65 percent of its asbestos. But as Table 14 indicates, by the mid-1970s, Canada's shares were down to 35 percent and 40 percent, respectively.

greater than 150 feet are also allowed for, reserves increase by about another 250 billion barrels, equal to 39 percent of world reserves of conventional crude.[10]

Current and Future Issues

As with the manufacturing sector — although perhaps of a more recent vintage — changes have been taking place, both domestically and abroad, that have altered the competitive position of Canada's mining sector and placed a number of challenges before the nation. These include a gradual erosion of Canada's comparative advantage in both crude mineral production and initial processing; the growing capital intensity of mineral production and, therefore, increasing demands for capital to sustain output; the problem of obtaining sufficient capital from domestic and foreign sources while ensuring that monopoly rents accrue to Canadians; and issues relating to domestic employment. Space does not permit a full analysis of these challenges, but at least they can be delineated briefly.

Declining Comparative Advantage

In our discussion it will be useful to separate the petroleum and natural gas industry from the rest of mining.

In mining *per se*, Canada appears to be losing some of the comparative advantage it once had, and productivity advances in the future may not be able to match the record since World War II. Because of the country's proximity to the United States and its political stability, Canada's more accessible, higher-quality resources have tended to be exploited more quickly than those in many developing lands. Simultaneously, the poorer countries have been actively encouraging large transnational corporations to develop and process their mineral resources, which are often more readily attainable and of exceptional quality.[11] To do this, they are frequently prepared to make a variety of types of concessions. To the extent that international development agencies provide cheap financing for resource exploitation, the trend is reinforced. Once mines are established through contractual arrangements or government participation, these nations tend to encourage production, even in periods of slack demand, and to undercut world prices to ensure the continued sales so necessary for generating export revenues and continued

---

[10]Other nations also have potential or actual non-conventional sources of oil: for example, both the United States and Estonia have oil shale. If these were all counted in world reserve estimates, the Canadian share would not, of course, be as great as indicated. We compare the Canadian oil sands resources to conventional world crude reserves merely to demonstrate their relative magnitude.

[11]Canada is now producing "some of the lowest grade ores in the world" (see H. C. Armstrong, "Investment in the Canadian Non-Fuels Minerals Industry," paper presented to the Canadian Group of the Trilateral Commission's Seminar on the Canadian Perspective on Commodities, Winnipeg, November 27-28, 1977, p. 10).

TABLE 14

Canadian Mineral Production and Reserves in a World Context, 1970-75

| | Canada in Relation to World | | | | Canada in Relation to Non-Communist Countries[a] | | | | |
| | Share of World Production, 1974-75 Average (%) | Share of Identified World Reserves,[b] 1975 (%) | Rank among World Producers, 1974-75 Average | Rank As Source of Identified World Reserves, 1975 | Share of Non-Communist Production, 1974 (%) | Share of Identified Non-Communist Reserves, 1974 (%) | Rank among Non-Communist Producers, 1974 | Rank As Source of Identified Non-Communist Reserves, 1974 | Canadian Share of U.S. Imports, 1970-73 Average (%) |
	(1)	(2)	(3)	(4)	(5)	(6)	(7)	(8)	(9)
Metals:									
Iron ore	5	14	6	2	8	19	5	2	51
Nickel	35	16	1	2	43	18	1	2	76
Cobalt	6	7	4	5	8	9	3	4	5
Columbium	13	8	2	2	13	8	2	2	1
Molybdenum	16	14	2	3	18	17	2	3	35
Tantalum	14[c]	7[c]	3[c]	3	14	7	3	3	23
Tungsten	3	12	6	2	10	40	4	1	35
Copper	11	9	3	4	13	11	3	3	34
Lead	10	10	4	4	13	12	3	3	30
Zinc	20	23	1	1	29	31	1	1	52
Germanium	6	[d]	5	[d]	6	[d]	4	[d]	n.a.
Gold	4	4	3	4	5	4	2	3	48
Mercury	4	2	7	7	7	3	5	6	53
Platinum group	7	2	3	3	12	4	2	2	1
Selenium	20	9	2	3	n.a.	11	2	3	89
Silver	14	12	2	4	18	18	1	3	44
Strontium	40	n.a.	1	n.a.	42	n.a.	1	n.a.	0
Uranium	19[e]	n.a.	2	3	20	23	2	2	80

Other minerals:									
Asbestos	40[f]	40	1	1	65	60	1	1	96
Fluorspar	3[f]	2	11	12	4	3	9	10	0
Potash	21[e]	n.a.	2		30	n.a.	1	n.a.	88
Petroleum and natural gas:									
Conventional crude[g]	2.3	.93	13	17	2.9	1.1	11	15	
Natural gas[g]		2.3				3.7			
Oil sands[h]		4.0				4.7			
Deposits		30.0				33.6			

n.a. = not available

[a] Including Yugoslavia.
[b] Identified reserves refer here to known reserves estimated to be economically recoverable at present (for more details see British-North American Committee, *Mineral Development in the Eighties*, pp. 30-31).
[c] There appeared to be an error in the first source regarding these figures, so the second source was used to correct it.
[d] Mostly recovered from zinc ores and coal ash, but estimates of reserves not available.
[e] 1973-74 average.
[f] 1974 production.
[g] For 1977.
[h] For 1974.

Sources: British-North American Committee, *Mineral Development in the Eighties: Prospects and Problems* (Montreal, Washington, D.C., and London, 1976), Table 2; International Economic Studies Institute, *Basic Data for Estimating U.S. Mineral Requirements and Availability: A Research Compendium* (Washington, D.C., 1976).

domestic advance.[12] Companies, anxious to recover their investment, tend to reduce extraction and initial processing elsewhere than in their newest plants. Lower anti-pollution standards in developing countries encourage this trend.[13]

Although, to date, the system of trading preferences for developing countries does not seem to have placed Canada at a major disadvantage relative to them in the initial processing of crude resource exports,[14] additional concessions of this type may be more disadvantageous for Canada in the future, unless the developed nations substantially reduce their escalated tariffs on higher stages of processing. Other pressures, in addition to the escalated tariffs of industrial countries, may favor the processing of minerals in these latter nations: the development of huge bulk carrier ships and accompanying freight-rate structures; the desire of transnational corporations to do their processing close to their large markets or to their R & D facilities (which, in turn, are usually close to their head offices); and general unemployment problems all may be influential. Finally, higher provincial taxes on the mining sector in the past five years have undoubtedly made new investments in Canada less attractive than previously and add to the pressures already mentioned for firms to turn to other countries.[15]

Hence, although Canada's relative productivity in the mining sector vis-à-vis developed nations alone, such as the United States, indicates that the nation continues to have a comparative advantage in crude mineral production,[16] the forces outlined above strongly

---

[12] For a discussion of this and other issues, see Winston G. Chambers, *Canadian Minerals and International Economic Interdependence,* Mineral Bulletin MR 162 (Ottawa: Energy, Mines and Resources Canada, 1976), and W. G. Chambers and J. S. Reid, "Canadian Resource Management and the North-South Dialogue," in Queen's University, Centre for Resource Studies, *Canada's Mineral Trade: Implications for the Balance of Payments and Economic Development,* Proceedings of the Third Policy Discussion Seminar, September 6-8, 1978 (Kingston, Ontario, 1978).

[13] It does not seem entirely coincidental that, for the Canadian nickel industry — chiefly Inco and Falconbridge — the alternative to spending many millions on new equipment to reduce sulfur-dioxide emissions was to reduce total production of nickel. In other words, with slack world demand necessitating some cutbacks in production, the obvious place for them to do so was in Canada.

[14] Vittorio Corbo and Oli Hawrylyshyn, "Canada's Trade Relations with Developing Countries," mimeographed study prepared for the Economic Council of Canada, Ottawa, 1977, Chap. 10.

[15] See John A. Hansuld, "Why in Canada?," *Canadian Mining Journal* 96 (April, 1975): 20-22. These factors, plus the continuing slump in world demand for a number of metals and low rates of return, have undoubtedly contributed to the fact that apart from molybdenum the expansion of metal reserves, common during the 1960s, has virtually been non-existent since 1974 (D. A. Cranstone, "Canadian Reserves of Seven Metals," *Canadian Mining Journal,* February, 1978).

[16] Dorothy Walters, *Canadian Income Levels and Growth: An International Perspective* (Ottawa: Economic Council of Canada, 1968). This study was updated by D. J. Daly in "Mineral Resources in the Canadian Economy: Macro-Economic Implications," in Carl E. Beigie and Alfred O. Hero, Jr., eds., *Natural Resources in U.S.-Canadian Relations,* Vol. 1, *The Evolution of Policies and Issues* (Boulder, Colo.: Westview

suggest that this advantage is being, and will continue to be, eroded in world markets generally, since the rapid expansion of production in developing countries is seen by these nations as a means of hastening their own economic advance. Of course, the attractiveness of locating mines and other facilities in developing countries will be reduced if periodic flare-ups of internal hostilities and the shutting off of production — as occurred in Zaire with respect to cobalt — are expected to become more common. This type of occurrence, however, does not seem an appropriate one to count on for the prosperity of Canada's mining sector. Difficulties in establishing additional mineral processing in Canada are also present.

The situation with regard to energy production is quite different from that for other mineral exploitation. Canada has not had a comparative advantage in oil or, until recently, in coal. However, the OPEC cartel has boosted oil and other fuel prices so much that production from Canadian oil sands and coal reserves is increasingly competitive with foreign fuel sources. Of course, if OPEC should collapse, which appears unlikely, the situation would alter radically, but for the foreseeable future the main concerns are those associated with ensuring that sufficient capital is invested in additional energy production in the years ahead to develop Canadian resources to meet Canada's needs and to reduce its oil import dependency.

Capital Requirements

The capital costs of extraction, transportation, and — where appropriate — initial processing of energy supplies particularly, but of mineral products generally, are rising dramatically, so that both capital/output and capital/labor ratios will soar. This trend is becoming apparent in the cost of new mines. Even medium-sized metal mines may now require a $100 million investment, and the expense of bringing nonferrous metal mines into production apparently has risen threefold in the past decade.[17] The trend is perhaps best portrayed by the $2 billion Syncrude oil sands plant, which, when operating, will employ only 2,500 plant workers and another 500 office and administrative staff and will have a capital/labor ratio of over $700,000 per worker — compared with $180,000 per worker for the entire mining and petroleum sector, and $47,000 for all goods-producing industries, in 1976 dollars. The proposed $4 billion heavy-oil plant for Cold Lake, when operating, will, in turn, have a capital/labor ratio of about $2 million.

Yet much of this investment is necessary. Canada's annual trade deficit in fossil fuels could be as great as $10 billion in 1990 if

---

Press for the C. D. Howe Research Institute and the World Peace Foundation, 1980), Chap. 5.

[17]See Armstrong, *op. cit.*, and "Bucking the Pessimistic Trend in Mining," *Business Week*, August 1, 1976, pp. 32-39.

major steps are not taken to make the nation more self-reliant in energy. To avoid this deficit, total energy investment during 1976-90 may have to be, cumulatively, over $180 billion in 1975 dollars.[18] Even if a conservative 5$1/2$ percent average rate of inflation is assumed, this sum would amount to about $300 billion in current dollars over the 15-year period. Whereas energy investments accounted for about 20 percent of industrial capital and for about 3 percent of GNE in the mid-1960s and rose to 30.6 percent and 4.6 percent, respectively, in 1976, for the late 1970s and the 1980s they are expected to account for 36-38 percent of industrial capital and 6-7 percent of GNP.[19]

In the non-fuel mineral sector the new investments required, although not as large as for energy production, are still quite substantial. If Canadian capacity is to grow at even one-half the growth rate achieved in 1960-75, outlays for exploration, new development of mines and smelters, and repair capital for existing mines and smelters must rise from current annual levels of about $2 billion in 1975 dollars to $6 billion by the year 2000.[20] For the 15 years 1976-90 these estimates imply nearly $50 billion of outlays in 1975 dollars. Investment in non-fuel minerals would rise from about one percent of GNE to 1.3 percent in the mid-1980s. Hence total energy and mineral investments could account for 8 percent of GNE by the mid- or late 1980s.

The scheduling of these massive investments is important. On the one hand, if they are not undertaken soon enough, additional supplies of minerals, especially of fossil fuels, will not be available when required. On the other hand, if too much is attempted at one time, it will lead to bottlenecks because of insufficient numbers of skilled tradesmen and insufficient domestic capacity to meet requirements for machinery, equipment, and other inputs. Thus greater imports of supplies, with correspondingly smaller domestic multiplier effects, will occur than if better scheduling had prevailed.

A weakness of focusing only on aggregate numbers is that it eschews questions relating to whether the necessary funds will be available and will move into the Canadian mineral and energy sectors through private market channels or whether greater government

---

[18]Energy, Mines and Resources Canada, *An Energy Strategy for Canada: Policies for Self-Reliance* (Ottawa, 1976).

[19]Toronto-Dominion Bank estimates (see Douglas D. Peters, "Energy Investment and the Canadian Economy," *Business and Economics* 6 [June, 1977]) assume a staged development so that energy investments would rise gradually as a percentage of GNE throughout the 1980s, to about 6.7 percent in 1990. The Royal Bank sees such investment amounting to 5 percent of GNE in the late 1970s, 6.8 percent in 1981-85, and 4.6 percent in 1986-90 (see Ralph Sultan, "Energy Finance," paper prepared for The Conference Board in Canada's Fourth Canadian Financial Conference, Montreal, June 28-29, 1977).

[20]Armstrong, *op. cit.*, p. 16.

direction and/or participation will be required.[21] For reasons mentioned earlier, non-energy mineral investment may tend to move to take advantage of opportunities in foreign countries. In the energy sector, however, the shift of funds abroad probably will be much less of a problem, as opportunities for additional investment in Canada are enormous. Moreover, the oil companies also appear willing and able to diversify outside their traditional areas of expertise into areas such as coal and uranium.[22] The main issues for this sector relate to whether the profits generated by higher energy prices should go to the largely foreign-owned oil industry to be reinvested to expand their ownership and control in Canada or whether governments and/or domestically owned firms should be the ones to benefit. We return to this subject in the next section.

As Canada shifts more of its investment away from producing other products in favor of new, high-cost energy production such as secondary and tertiary recovery of conventional oil and gas, deeper horizon and frontier drilling, heavy oil, and oil sands, labor productivity will be reduced. More labor and capital will be required to produce a given unit of energy. And because energy is an input into other products, there will be an adverse effect upon productivity in the rest of the economy as well.[23] An unfavorable impact upon Canadian real income would still arise even if Canada attempted to focus on increasing its exports of other goods, such as minerals, forestry and agricultural products, and manufactures, in exchange for energy from abroad. The rapidly rising foreign price of oil means that, for each barrel imported, Canada has to export more of these other commodities (thus requiring more labor and capital), so that domestic real income is again reduced. In the economist's terms, this is the untoward terms-of-trade effect of higher-priced energy imports.[24]

Economic Rents and Foreign Ownership

Another issue intertwined with that of adequate capital supplies has to do with appropriating economic rents from non-replenishable natural resources. The firms involved in finding and extracting resources need to obtain a return on their investment, adjusted for risk, at least equivalent to what they can obtain in other industries or in

---

[21] The projected extent of total capital inflows required to meet future Canadian current-account deficits was discussed in Chapter 3.

[22] For a somewhat less optimistic view on this issue, see Sultan, *op. cit.,* pp. 15-16.

[23] Department of Finance, *The Effects of Higher Energy Prices on Long-Run Growth* (Ottawa, 1978).

[24] *Ibid.* Also note that estimates have been made of how higher energy prices reduce consumer expenditures. Anthony P. Ellison (*The Effects of Rising Energy Costs on Canadian Industries* [Calgary: Canadian Energy Research Institute, 1979], p. 39) states that "a comparison of the short and the long run price elasticity measures shows that a doubling of the prices of the primary energy commodities is likely to reduce total final consumer expenditure in the short run by 1.9 percent and in the long run by 6.5 percent."

the same industry in other countries. Returns over and above this necessary reward are usually referred to as economic rents. It is these rents in which it is generally thought that the citizens of a nation are entitled to share.

There are, however, great difficulties in determining the magnitude of available rents, given that ore bodies and oil and gas pools differ with regard to such things as size and quality, the combination of minerals present, the costs of development, and the costs involved in moving equipment and supplies to, and the product from, the site. Continual changes in world demand and supply conditions occur as well — as, indeed, they have done over the past decade. Added to these problems is the question of how to divide the economic rents between the provincial and federal governments. The corporations may be squeezed in this intergovernmental struggle.[25]

It is no easy task to determine the economic rents for any one mine or oil pool, let alone to construct a standardized tax structure to appropriate all, or a majority of, the rents, on the one hand, and to avoid, on the other hand, dipping into the return required for the investment to take place at all and for new domestic exploration to continue as desired.

An additional complication arises because of the large amount of foreign ownership of Canada's mining sector.[26] In the case of Canadian-owned firms, any rents not obtained directly for the benefit of the populace as a whole at least end up with Canadian shareholders or Canadian companies to reinvest at home or abroad. Even if Canadian firms invest abroad, Canada obtains the benefit of dividends and other monies remitted to head offices or to other Canadian residents. And if tax rates are equal at home and abroad, and a choice exists as to where to take profits, there will be a natural tendency to take them in the home office. Thus they will be subject to domestic corporate and personal income taxes and thereby be to the benefit of the entire nation.

But with foreign-owned corporations, a failure to appropriate the economic rents means that they either go to foreign shareholders directly or increase foreign investment in the Canadian economy and raise the level of dividends and other payouts to foreign shareholders in the future. Higher resource prices can then mean —

---

[25] In the late 1960s, and particularly in the very early 1970s, the demand for minerals, and the resulting prices, was strong, and profits were high. The industry expanded and, in so doing, incurred much new debt. As profits rose, corporate taxes as a share of before-tax profits — which had been disproportionately low for the mineral sector compared with other sectors such as manufacturing — were increased. The provinces raised their royalty rates too, so that some estimates suggested that marginal tax rates in some jurisdictions were greater than 100 percent. In 1974 and subsequently, demand for many metals slumped, and so did profits. Recovery of demand for many metals is still far from complete.

[26] See note 8 above.

as they have meant on occasion, and mean now with respect to oil and gas particularly — that if the rents are not extracted by domestic tax systems, Canadians end up paying foreign shareholders more to consume their own resources.[27] It is also possible for foreign-owned firms to minimize profits, and hence taxes, in Canada by their control of the prices at which products are shipped between subsidiaries and parents, and vice versa, and by a range of other charges for management fees, technology, and so forth. The data for the metal-mining industry for 1972-76 are certainly consistent with this possibility. In each of these five years three different measures of profit rates indicate that foreign-owned firms consistently had substantially lower profits than did the Canadian-owned sector of the industry. The foreign rates of return averaged only 36 percent of those reported by Canadian-owned firms.[28] One might argue that all that this shows is that foreign-owned mining firms are much less efficient than are Canadian-owned firms. However, this hypothesis does not fit with the commonly held view that foreign-owned firms are generally at the forefront of managerial skills and technology. Even if it is true, it suggests that, in terms of efficient performance — quite apart from the matter of ease of extracting economic rents — there is a case to be made for greater domestic ownership of the mineral industry.[29]

These remarks indicate that the capturing of economic rents for society's benefit is easier, the more the industry is domestically owned and controlled. One might observe, too, that, if minerals are processed beyond their crude forms within Canada, the appropriating of rents is easier as well; for if the rents are not picked up at the

---

[27] One recent study addressing this foreign-ownership issue suggested that, for every $1.00 per barrel increase in the price of "old" oil (that is, oil found prior to the OPEC price increases commencing in 1973), Canadians pay 21 cents. This is after making generous allowance for corporate income taxes and possible withholding taxes, which may be paid by foreign oil companies! If the oil price were raised $10 a barrel, then at current rates of production the cost to Canadians would be about $1.4 billion annually. Even without any *additional* price increases, there are large economic rents being drained off by the foreign oil companies. These could be running at between $1 billion and $1.4 billion a year. (See B. Wilkinson and B. Scarfe, "The Recycling Problem," paper prepared for the Ontario Economic Council Energy Conference, Toronto, September 27-28, 1979.)

[28] See Appendix Table A.5.

[29] One curious, and unconvincing, defense of foreign ownership of the minerals industry has been made by D. J. Daly (*op. cit.*), who attempts to suggest that the lower profit rates of foreign-owned firms compared to Canadian-owned firms, accompanied by their lower wages and salaries as a proportion of sales, imply that foreign-owned firms "out-performed" Canadian-owned firms because their value added was less, relative to output — even though their consumption of materials and other inputs was greater, relative to output! One does not often see a high cost of inputs and other expenses as a percentage of sales offered as a sign of superior performance. Daly perfunctorily dismisses the possibility that high input costs and low profit rates may have something to do with transfer pricing and other intracompany charges that are possible with foreign ownership. It is also surprising to see low profit rates applauded as a partial justification of foreign ownership.

mining stage, there remains the possibility they will be at the smelting, refining, and subsequent processing stages.

An issue closely associated with that of ensuring that the economic rents from Canadian resources accrue to Canadian citizens in general, and with the need for large new investments, is that of ensuring that the value of these rents, which are a part of society's capital, is not entirely spent on expanding consumption today but is suitably invested to reap returns to future generations. Clearly, revenue collected on the production of non-replaceable resources can be, and should be, at least in part, a source of funds for new investments now and in the future.[30]

Employment

Although the capital and investment needs of the mineral sector are huge and are probably going to absorb a greater share of GNE and total investment, a question arises as to the effectiveness of such investment in contributing to a reduction in domestic unemployment. In the initial investment or construction phase, the employment effects are about double those of an equivalent investment in manufacturing. However, over the lifetime of the projects, taking into account direct and indirect employment expansion as well as the induced employment from additional consumer spending as a consequence of the extra income paid to the household sector, investment in the mineral industry would expand employment by only one-quarter of that which an equal investment in manufacturing would provide.[31] In other words, although the very short-run

---

[30]The Alberta Heritage Savings Trust Fund, into which flow roughly one-third of the province's oil revenues and which at the end of 1978 totaled about $4.2 billion, appears to be an attempt to provide funds for present and future investment (see B. L. Scarfe and T. L. Powrie, "The Optimal Savings Question: An Alberta Perspective," paper prepared for the Alberta Heritage Savings Trust Fund, University of Alberta, October 18-19, 1979, forthcoming in *Canadian Public Policy*).

[31]See J. E. Stahl and D. J. McCulla, *The Canadian Mineral Industry and Economic Development* (Ottawa: Energy, Mines and Resources Canada, 1975), Table 23, pp. 40-52 (the total GNE generated over the life of each project will be three times larger for the manufacturing investment). An earlier study by M. W. Bucovetsky ("A Study of the Role of the Resource Industries in the Canadian Economy," Working Paper No. 7301 [Toronto: Institute for the Quantitative Analysis of Social and Economic Policy, University of Toronto, 1973]) concluded that there was not much difference between the employment effects of investment in mining and those of investment in manufacturing. However, his study did not allow, as it should have, for induced employment effects from the extra consumer spending generated by the process.

Note also that another study by McCulla ("Minerals and the Canadian Development Process," in Queen's University, Centre for Resource Studies, *Canadian Mineral Trade, the Balance of Payments and Economic Development*, Proceeding No. 4 [Kingston, Ontario, 1978], p. 47) concluded that "development stimulation is greatest at the third stage [semi-fabricating], followed by the second for metals [metallurgical extraction such as smelting, refining, and leaching], with the first stage [mining and concentration] providing the least stimulation."

effects of additional investment in the mining sector appear favorable compared with those of investment in the construction of new plants in manufacturing (which involves a large import component), the more permanent employment effects are much less from mining ventures.

Also note that employment exhibits much more year-to-year instability in the mining sector than in industry as a whole.[32] Once construction of new installations is complete, employment drops off dramatically. Moreover, the opening of new mines is an irregular occurrence. Hence emphasizing crude mineral exploitation alone not only involves smaller long-run employment benefits but also contributes to the instability of employment in general.[33]

A final question is whether workers with the requisite skills will be available in sufficient numbers when they are needed. This question relates back to the matter of appropriate planning and scheduling of new investments so that training and/or retraining programs are possible. Tied in with this issue is the perennial one plaguing mineral development in remote regions — a labor turnover that is much higher than average when compared with the rest of the economy.[34] If more rapid mineral development occurs, these concerns may become of growing importance.

Concluding Remarks

A number of concerns have been raised regarding further non-replenishable resource development in Canada:

- increasing relative dependence upon crude materials in mineral exports;

- declining comparative advantage as resource exploitation proceeds in foreign countries;

- the availability of capital;

- the timing of investment;

- the need to provide incentives for private capital while obtaining and using in the best interests of society the economic rents from these resources;

- the employment effects of such development.

---

[32] Economic Council of Canada, *Toward More Stable Growth in Construction* (Ottawa, 1974), pp. 108-09.

[33] It is true that business cycles in Canada have been less severe than in the United States, but this is despite, not because of, Canada's heavy reliance upon crude mineral exploitation and exports (see Derek White, *Business Cycles in Canada* [Ottawa: Economic Council of Canada, 1967]).

[34] See F. A. Macmillan, G. S. Gislason, and S. Lyon, *Human Resources in Canadian Mining: A Preliminary Analysis* (Kingston, Ontario: Centre for Resource Studies, Queen's University, 1977), Chap. 6.

These issues suggest that the continued contribution of the mineral sector to Canadian development should not be taken for granted.

Before concluding this section, it is perhaps appropriate to mention that the basic physical adequacy of Canada's mineral reserves, at least over the next fifteen years — and for some minerals, much longer — is not the vital issue. It is true that for some minerals the better-quality, more easily exploitable reserves are becoming scarce and that higher prices will be necessary in the longer run to make their extraction economically feasible, especially because of exponentially rising energy costs as lower-grade deposits are tapped. But known nickel and iron deposits are probably sufficient for domestic and export needs to at least the year 2000, as are reserves of asbestos and potash. Up to 1990, reserves of copper, zinc, lead, and molybdenum are expected to meet just about all requirements, although by that time new sources (that is, supplies other than from existing mines and known undeveloped deposits whose future development appears likely) will have to be called upon to some extent and by 2000 will have to provide about 50 percent of total needs.[35] But the evidence suggests that the earth's crust contains far larger supplies of these minerals than was once anticipated.[36]

Fossil fuel deposits in Canada are immense. Coal reserves in Alberta and British Columbia (although coal is not a "clean" fuel) and the oil sands and heavy oil in Alberta and Saskatchewan, quite apart from possible new reserves of conventional crude oil and natural gas in the foothills of Alberta and in northern and eastern offshore frontiers, are adequate to meet Canadian domestic needs for decades. For most minerals for which Canada already has an established world position, physical availability is not, therefore, in itself expected to be the major problem. (This is even true with respect to uranium,[37] for large new sources have been found in northern Saskatchewan.)[38] Much more pressing are the other issues indicated above, as well as the seemingly perpetual one of limiting the pollution of the environment.[39]

---

[35] These estimates are from Energy, Mines and Resources Canada, Mineral Development Sector, *Mineral Area Planning Study* (Ottawa, 1975).

[36] See G. J. S. Govett and M. H. Govett, eds., *World Mineral Supplies: Assessment and Perspective* (New York: Elsemier Scientific Publishing, 1976).

[37] Energy, Mines and Resources Canada (*op. cit.*) expected uranium to be a mineral in short supply in Canada if exports were not curtailed.

[38] See, for example, John Soganich, "It Might Be the Largest Uranium Find in the World," *Financial Post*, October 14, 1978.

[39] At the world level it is also believed that the physical supply of non-replenishable resources is not the main concern. Rather, the chief need is to be able to develop an "inexhaustible, nonpolluting source of energy" that can be used to assist in the process of substitution of one raw material for another. "In the Age of Substitutability energy is the ultimate raw material. The living standard will almost surely depend primarily on the cost of prime energy." (H. E. Goeller and Alvin M. Weinberg, "The Age of Substitutability," *American Economic Review* 68 [December, 1978]: 9-10.)

Agriculture

Productivity

As noted earlier, a sizable proportion of the improvement in average labor productivity in the economy during the two decades immediately following World War II was attributable to the huge shift of workers from agriculture into the manufacturing and service industries. Moreover, although agricultural productivity per worker still remained much below that of most other sectors, the pace of improvement exceeded that in most other sectors.[40] Much of the gain, however, was simply from more capital — primarily machinery — being employed per worker. Inputs affecting crop and livestock yields — such as better seed varieties, pesticides, and fertilizers — were less than half as significant as inputs of extra equipment. Other contributors to the productivity increase came from such factors as better farm management, larger farms, and product specialization.[41]

Despite advances in Canada's agricultural productivity, output per worker in Canada remains roughly 80 percent of that in the United States. In contrast to Canadian gains, U.S. improvements depended more on the expansion of outlays affecting yield technology and less on additional machinery and equipment. Noteworthy too is the fact that the United States devoted to research about twice the staff per million acres of wheat production as did Canada.[42]

In the decade up to about 1974, productivity growth in Canada was less than in the earlier two decades and, depending upon the time periods, sectors, and regions selected for comparison, was minimal or negative. Augmentation emanated primarily from the additional inputs — particularly capital equipment — being combined with labor.[43] With better grain crops in the years since 1974, total output indexes have strengthened, so that productivity growth has tended to regain a little of the vitality it had in the early 1960s,[44] although Canada still remains well behind the United States.

International Trade and Comparative Advantage

The general structure of Canada's trade in agricultural products has altered little over the years, at least in terms of the relative

---

[40] See our discussion in Chapter 2.

[41] L. Auer, "Labour Productivity in Agriculture: A Canada-U.S. Comparison," *Canadian Journal of Agricultural Economics* 18 (November, 1970): 43-55.

[42] *Ibid.*, p. 50.

[43] D. M. Shute, "National and Regional Productivity of Canadian Agriculture, 1961 to 1974," *Canadian Farm Economics* 10 (December, 1975): 1-6.

[44] See United Nations Food and Agriculture Organization (FAO), *Production Yearbook,* 1976 (Rome, 1977), Table 4. Canada's food production per capita in 1974 was actually only 90 percent of its 1961-65 average, but by 1976 this figure had recovered to 113 percent — roughly the same as the corresponding ratio for the world (110 percent).

TABLE 15

Canadian Trade Balances on Agricultural Commodity Groups, 1951-78
(million current dollars)

	1951	1961	1966	1971	1976	1978
	(1)	(2)	(3)	(4)	(5)	(6)
Grains and grain products	668	738	1,173	1,094	2,388	2,467
(wheat and wheat flour)	(555)	(724)	(1,144)	(885)	(1,830)	(2,063)
Oilseeds and oilseed products	–39	11	17	122	15	354
Animal feeds	25	12	30	46	74	94
Animals, meat, and meat products	87	48	78	40	–80	90
Dairy products	7	16	17	44	4	0
Poultry and eggs	–1	–7	–11	0	–45	10
Fruits, vegetables, and nuts	–121	–230	–251	–359	–717	–1,085
Other[a]	–319	–210	–229	–293	–805	–972
	307	378	824	694	834	958

[a]Includes seeds for sowing, honey, sugar, tobacco, vegetable fibers, plantation crops, and all other agricultural products.

Sources: 1951-76: Department of Agriculture, Economics Branch, *Canada's Trade in Agricultural Products* (Ottawa, 1977).
1978: Statistics Canada, *Exports by Commodities* and *Imports by Commodities* (Ottawa, 1978).

importance of net trade in the various commodity groups (see Table 15). The dominant net export item continues to be wheat, with exports of other grains being of much lesser magnitude. Net trade in animal feeds, although positive, remains relatively insignificant. Growth in the production and export of oilseeds (rapeseed) and oilseed products has been the major new development during the past decade (exports amounted to $480 million in 1978), but continued expansion of imports, especially from the United States, of processed products has, at least until recently, prevented this sector from making any consistent, large contribution to a positive trade balance. Huge and swelling deficits are occurring in fruits, vegetables, and nuts, as well as in items such as sugar.

It is customary to think of Canada as having a major comparative advantage in agricultural products, but if the structure of the nation's trade balance for this sector is any indication, that comparative advantage is based upon one product group — grains, and particularly unmilled wheat. There is scope for an improved international competitive position in oilseeds and oilseed products and possibly animal feeds — or even live animals, meat, and meat products, provided the Canadian dollar remains at or below its current level of about U.S.$0.85. However, a restoration of the Canadian dollar to something near parity with the U.S. dollar would effectively prevent much, if any, improvement from occurring in the trade balance in this sector. The low, erratic rainfall on the Prairies, the short growing season, and the cold weather — not to mention the less efficient organization and management of production (although, as indicated earlier, improvements are continually being made in this regard) — all raise production costs, especially vis-à-vis the United States. As for dairy and poultry products, only import restrictions enable these industries to survive. Also, Canada's policy of encouraging marketing boards for various meat, poultry, and dairy products sometimes seems designed to defend the status quo rather than to systematically enhance efficiency and competitiveness in world markets.[45] The huge and multiplying trade deficits in fruits, vegetables, nuts, and sugar and other plantation products reflect the unsuitability of the Canadian climate for producing some of these products, the shortness of season in which the rest of them can be grown, and the positive effect of higher incomes on the demand for fresh — as opposed to stored — products. Exchange rate changes will have a fairly small effect on these deficits.[46]

Recall, as well, that the processing of food products has been one of the more highly protected segments of Canadian manufacturing, that this sector is quite unskilled-labor-intensive, and that the developing nations desire to process more of their products prior to export.[47] Note too that, even with grains, where Canada has a strong position, future market expansion is limited because of such things as the heavy — and unlikely to be reduced — agricultural protectionism of the EEC and Japan, with the accompanying subsidization of surplus product exports to other lands; the limited purchasing power of the impoverished nations; the increasing potential of nations such as Brazil to become net grain exporters; the spasmodic (according to the state of their domestic harvests) nature of purchases by such countries as the U.S.S.R.; and finally, on the supply side, the difficulties of substantially increasing Canadian exports, given the limitations on suitable land and on the benefits derivable

---

[45] Herbert Grubel and Richard Schwindt, *The Real Cost of the B.C. Milk Board: A Case Study in Canadian Agriculture Policy* (Vancouver: The Fraser Institute, 1977).

[46] For more extensive treatment of many of the issues raised in this discussion, see David Kirk, "Some Aspects of Canadian Agricultural Trade Issues," study prepared for the Trilateral Commission Canadian Group's Commodities and Trade Seminar, Winnipeg, November 27-28, 1977; T. K. Warley, *Agriculture in an Interdependent World: U.S. and Canadian Perspectives* (Montreal and Washington, D.C.: Canadian-American Committee, 1977); Richard Shaffner, *HRI Observations,* No. 14, *The Quest for Farm Income Stability in Canada* (Montreal: C. D. Howe Research Institute, 1977); M. M. Veeman and T. S. Veeman, "The Changing Organization, Structure and Control of Canadian Agriculture," *American Journal of Agricultural Economics* 60, No. 5 (December, 1978): 759-68; and Organisation for Economic Cooperation and Development (OECD), *Study of Trends in World Supply and Demand of Major Agricultural Commodities* (Paris, 1976).

[47] See Chapter 4 (particularly Table 9) and R. M. A. Lyons and R. L. Louks, eds., *Competition and Public Policy on Competition in the Canadian Food Industry: Proceedings of Agricultural and Food Marketing Forum* (Winnipeg: Department of Agricultural Economics and Farm Management, University of Manitoba, 1977).

from applying more capital and other inputs, and from the increases in domestic demand as the population grows.[48] Finally, the general confusion regarding what Canadian food production policies are supposed to be accomplishing, or should accomplish, adds to the skepticism one must have about major improvements occurring in Canada's presently very restricted comparative advantage in agricultural products or in the growth of this sector in general.

Forest Products

The forest products sector accounts for about 12 percent of manufacturing employment and 15 percent of manufacturing value added and is about 40 percent foreign-owned.[49] It is the largest net earner of foreign exchange of any sector in Canada. The three chief products, making up nearly 90 percent of all forest products exports, are softwood lumber, wool pulp, and newsprint[50] — all products involving a relatively small amount of domestic processing prior to export and facing zero or low foreign tariffs.

Projections of, and expectations regarding, the future of these items are fairly modest. Softwood lumber sales abroad are primarily to the United States and depend largely upon the cyclical state of U.S. housing construction. World consumption is forecast to grow at only 2-3 percent a year.[51] World markets for paper (and paperboard), which have been rising at about 5 percent annually over the past 25 years, are anticipated to grow more slowly over the next 10-15 years — at about $3^1/_2$ percent annually — and the market for newsprint is expected to grow even more slowly. Canada may have to accept a smaller share of this market, since much new pulp capacity is being constructed to utilize both the large southern pine forests of the United States (which are highly accessible and regenerate within 20 years compared with as much as 60 years for spruce and fir in Canada) and the softwoods in Latin America (which mature within 15-20 years). Anti-pollution requirements are imposing heavy capital costs on the pulp and paper industry, and concern has been expressed as to whether, without adequate tax concessions, the investment climate will be as favorable in Canada as abroad. The forest products sector is the biggest industrial consumer of energy in Canada, so that energy costs are important to it. Yet it could generate fairly

---

[48] Issues have also been raised regarding the effect on soil quality of continuous cropping with heavy fertilizer applications and the loss of good land to urbanization, road building, and low-density rural living. For an easy-to-read review of a variety of questions, see Canadian Imperial Bank of Commerce, "Canada's Food Land Resource," *Commercial Letter* 3 (1977).

[49] Department of Industry, Trade and Commerce, *Report of the Consultative Task Force on the Forest Products Industry* (Ottawa, 1978), Appendix 1, p. 3.

[50] In 1978 the relative shares were lumber, 33 percent; wood pulp, 23 percent; and newsprint, 30 percent.

[51] The remainder of this paragraph draws on Department of Industry, Trade and Commerce, *op. cit.*, particularly Appendix 1.

cheaply a sizable share of its energy needs from its waste products, provided anti-pollution requirements are not so expensive as to discourage the use of this replenishable energy supply. R & D expenditure as a percentage of industry sales has been declining and is now less than that of Canada's major competitors — the United States and the Scandinavian countries. What R & D is done is insufficiently directed toward market needs.

These brief remarks suggest that, while there can be little doubt that the chief forest products will continue to make a substantial contribution to Canadian output, employment, and exports, there is much scope for improvement in the performance of this sector if Canada's position in world markets is to be maintained. The depreciation of the Canadian dollar in 1977-78, while greatly strengthening this sector's international competitive position (after its erosion in the mid-1970s), can hardly be expected to obviate adaptation and amelioration with respect to the continuing weaknesses the sector may have.

Other segments of the industry are not in even as favorable a position as these main exports. For example, fine papers and other specialty paper and wood products suffer considerably from a fragmented domestic structure and a need for modernization. (No new fine-paper machine has been put in place in Canada during the past ten years.)[52] The posture of these segments is similar to that of much of Canadian manufacturing, as discussed in Chapter 4.

Concluding Comments

This brief survey of productivity developments and/or changes in comparative advantage for the Canadian resource products sector suggests that, although this sector is traditionally where Canada's international trading strength has resided, the scope for significant new gains is limited. At least it may be difficult to make major new gains. We next turn to setting this discussion in the broader framework of Canada's overall balance of international payments.

---

[52]*Ibid.*, Appendix 1, p. 11.

6

The Balance of Payments

Introduction

A number of references have been made in earlier chapters to relationships between Canada's internal growth and its external competitive position. For a nation that depends upon foreign trade for 25 percent of its GNE, these relationships are clearly of vital importance. It is useful at this juncture, therefore, to provide a summary review of Canada's balance of payments position over time. We begin by focusing on the merchandise trade account and then take up the remaining components of the balance of payments.

Merchandise Trade

As indicated in Table 16, Canada's merchandise trade account was in deficit throughout most of the 1950s. Massive capital imports, accompanied by imports of investment goods in the first part of the decade, and then recession in both Canada and the United States, together with inappropriate monetary and fiscal policies in Canada that kept the floating Canadian dollar valued above parity with the U.S. dollar, were largely responsible for this situation. During the 1960s the depreciation of the dollar from 1960 to 1962 to a pegged rate of U.S.$0.925, as well as a number of other domestic and world developments mentioned in Chapter 4, helped to stimulate exports of manufactured goods.

The peak year of surplus in Canada's merchandise account, at least until 1978, was 1970. The performance that year was partially the result of special circumstances in 1969 that caused delays in some exports until 1970[1] and the temporary elimination of the previous huge deficits in automotive trade with the United States

---

[1] A number of strikes that year in several raw materials and fabricating industries — iron, nickel, copper, and steel — resulted in exports' being below what they otherwise would have been — by anywhere from $250 million to $350 million. Also, previous lethargy in wheat sales was being overcome in part. For an expanded discussion see B. Wilkinson, "The Canadian Balance of Payments," in K. Acheson, J. Chant, and G. Paquet, eds., *Canadian Perspectives in Economics* (Toronto: Collier-Macmillan, 1972).

TABLE 16

**Canada's Merchandise Trade Balance
with the World and with the United States, 1950-78**
(million Canadian dollars)

	World	United States
1950	7	-50
1951	-151	-520
1952	485	-473
1953	-60	-590
1954	18	-440
1955	-211	-685
1956	-728	1,167
1957	-594	-947
1958	-176	-532
1959	-421	-536
1960	-148	-673
1961	173	-615
1962	184	-438
1963	503	-488
1964	701	-808
1965	118	-1,041
1966	224	-993
1967	566	-569
1968	1,471	389
1969	964	472
1970	3,052	1,121
1971	2,563	1,445
1972	1,857	1,513
1973	2,720	1,227
1974	1,519	1,002
1975	-534	-1,125
1976	1,089	393
1977	2,907	1,706
1978	3,468	2,367

Sources: Statistics Canada, *The Canadian Balance of International Payments, 1973-1974* (Ottawa, 1977) and *Quarterly Estimates of the Canadian Balance of International Payments* (Ottawa, various issues).

resulting from the auto pact. But in the spring of 1970, surging exports and large long-term capital inflows (which had commenced in 1969 in response to a stiff anti-inflationary, tight-money policy) put pressure on the authorities to free the Canadian dollar to float upward. (Ironically, Canada was simultaneously restricted in the extent to which it could permit short-term capital outflows — which would have reduced the pressure on the Canadian dollar — because of a commitment to discourage such outflows that had been given to the United States in 1968 in return for an exemption from U.S. restrictions on foreign direct investment announced January 1, 1968.) Over the nine months following the freeing of the Canadian exchange rate on June 1, 1970, the Canadian dollar floated upward to, or above, parity with the U.S. dollar. In the process the exchange rate advantage that Canadian products, especially manufactures, had been enjoying over U.S. products was eliminated. Any benefits in keeping Canada competitive that had resulted from the country's anti-inflationary policy of 1969 (which had, in turn, been precipitated by the explosive monetary expansion of 1967-68) were canceled out.

Thereafter, although Canada's merchandise trade surpluses generally remained quite large, in dollar terms, by historical standards, the basis for their strength was altering. Trade in automotive products swung sharply into deficit after 1972, reaching a peak of $1.9 billion in 1975 (it was still $0.8 billion in 1978); and the volume of manufactured imports (both fabricated materials and end products) began to rise more rapidly than the volume of exports (see Appendix Table A.6). However, petroleum and natural gas exports to the United States surged, and grain export revenues grew greatly in response to unusually favorable world markets. Favorable terms of trade from 1972 onward — especially for grains, metals, and other minerals — further helped to sustain export receipts for a few years.

Although Canada's merchandise account with the world had shifted to a surplus position in 1961, deficits in trade with the United States persisted until 1968. In fact, apart from a minute surplus in 1945, Canada experienced a trade deficit with the United States every year of this century until 1968. Then, it did not experience another deficit until 1975.

With this overview in mind, we turn now to some of the more detailed characteristics of Canadian trade.

Trade by Country and by Commodity

Changes in Canada's international trade between 1964 and 1978 are summarized in Table 17. The United States clearly dominates as a market for Canadian exports and as a supplier of Canadian imports. The most significant shifts in merchandise trade flows include the following:

TABLE 17

Destinations of Exports and Sources of Imports, Canada, 1964 and 1978
(percentages)

	United States		Japan		United Kingdom		EEC[a]		OPEC[b]		Rest of World	
	1964	1978	1964	1978	1964	1978	1964	1978	1964	1978	1964	1978
	(1)	(2)	(3)	(4)	(5)	(6)	(7)	(8)	(9)	(10)	(11)	(12)
Share of total Canadian exports	52.8	70.2	4.1	5.9	13.8	3.8	6.9	5.5	1.1	2.8	21.3	11.8
Share of highly manufactured Canadian exports[c]	54.1	81.6	1.6	0.7	6.6	1.6	8.1	2.5	1.6	5.1	27.9	8.5
Share of total Canadian imports	69.0	70.5	2.3	4.6	8.2	3.2	5.4	6.1	4.8	6.0	10.3	9.6
Share of highly manufactured Canadian imports[c]	78.9	78.9	2.1	5.3	8.2	3.2	5.8	6.3	0	0	5.0	6.3

[a]Excluding the United Kingdom.
[b]Abu Dhabi, Algeria, Ecuador, Gabon, Indonesia, Iran, Iraq, Kuwait, Libya, Nigeria, Qatar, Saudi Arabia, and Venezuela.
[c]Including the "end products" category of the *Trade of Canada* classification, plus chemicals (see Statistics Canada, *Trade of Canada Commodity Classification* [Ottawa, 1972]).

Source: Statistics Canada, *Summary of External Trade*, various issues.

- a much expanded proportion of total exports going to the United States and, to a lesser extent, to Japan and the OPEC nations, with offsetting declines occurring in shipments to the United Kingdom (because of its sluggish growth and its entry into the EEC, which eliminated the preferential tariff position Canada had had in U.K. markets), the EEC, and the rest of the world;
- a larger share of highly manufactured exports, directed primarily to the United States and the OPEC nations;
- Japan, the EEC, and OPEC becoming increasingly important suppliers to Canada, the first two of highly manufactured goods and the latter of petroleum;
- the United Kingdom fading as a Canadian supplier.

Other basic characteristics of Canadian trade are that

- raw and semi-fabricated materials comprise 60 percent of total Canadian exports and 95 percent, 82 percent, 82 percent, 62 percent, and 53 percent, respectively, of Canadian exports to Japan, the United Kingdom, the EEC (excluding the United Kingdom), the rest of the world, and the United States, with these percentages having increased over the past 14 years with respect to Japan and the EEC (see Appendix Table A.7);
- highly manufactured products account for 67 percent of total imports and 76 percent, 79 percent, 67 percent, and 69 percent, respectively, of imports from the United States, Japan, the United Kingdom, and the EEC (excluding the United Kingdom), with an expansion of these percentages having occurred with respect to all these nations since 1964 (see Appendix Table A.8).

Canada has not been as successful as other high-income countries in acquiring markets in developing nations. In 1978, the industrial countries as a whole made about 25 percent of their total foreign shipments to developing countries, whereas Canada had less than 10 percent of its export sales in these nations.[2]

Details of Canadian exports, by commodity group, as a share of the exports of each group by the major countries of the Western world provide additional insight into Canada's trade (see Table 18). Canada's share of OECD exports grew modestly between 1964 and 1967, primarily because of the swell in automotive and energy exports but also because of growth in the relative importance of exports of agricultural machinery and equipment and other machinery, apparatus, and appliances — primarily to the United States. Beginning in the 1970s, however, Canada's share diminished rather dramatically. By 1976 only energy products (petroleum and natural gas to the United States and coal to Japan) comprised a substantially larger share of total OECD exports of such products.

---

[2] Statistics Canada, *Summary of External Trade*, December, 1978 (Ottawa, 1979); General Agreement on Tariffs and Trade, Press Release, February 9, 1979, p. 3.

TABLE 18

**Canadian Exports As Percentages of OECD Exports,
by Commodity Group, 1964, 1967, and 1976**

	1964	1967	1976
	(1)	(2)	(3)
a) Food, beverages, and animal products and feeds	10.9	8.9	6.2
b) Wood and paper products	35.3	31.9	23.9
c) Crude minerals (except energy products)	33.5	34.0	27.6
d) Energy products	9.5	11.9	16.7
e) Iron and steel	3.2	2.9	2.3
f) Nonferrous semi-processed metals	24.7	23.3	15.0
g) Automobiles and parts	2.0	12.9	11.7
h) Agricultural machinery and equipment	7.8	9.5	7.3
i) Other machinery, apparatus, and appliances	2.6	3.3	2.3
j) Chemicals	2.7	2.9	2.5
k) Textiles	.7	.7	.6
l) Other manufactures	1.8	1.5	1.4
	7.1	7.5	6.1

Note: a) = SITC 0, 1, 21, 22, 29, 4
     b) = SITC 24, 25, 63, 64
     c) = SITC 27, 28
     d) = SITC 3
     e) = SITC 67
     f) = SITC 68
     g) = SITC 732
     h) = SITC 712
     i) = SITC 7 (except 712 and 732)
     j) = SITC 5
     k) = SITC 26, 65
     l) = SITC 61, 62, 8, 9.

Source: Organisation for Economic Co-operation and Development, *Market Summaries: Exports*, 1976 (Paris, 1978), Series C.

Canada's share of world exports diminished over the 1970s. It amounted to 5.3 percent in 1971 but only to 3.9 percent in 1975-77.[3] Perhaps more significantly, even though Canada's unit labor costs in manufacturing rose less, relative to most other developed countries, after 1967, the relative position of its highly manufactured exports in the markets of these nations also fell (see Appendix Table

---

[3] Economic Council of Canada, *Fifteenth Annual Review: A Time for Reason* (Ottawa, 1978), Table 2.1, p. 22.

A.9). Recently, a major reason for the lower unit labor costs has been the relative depreciation of the Canadian dollar vis-à-vis other currencies. Between mid-1976 and mid-1978 the Japanese yen and the West German mark rose by 59 percent and 42 percent, respectively, in terms of Canadian dollars. Yet from 1976 to 1978 the volume of exports of Canadian finished goods (that is, manufactured end products) to Japan and to the EEC excluding the United Kingdom (of which West Germany forms the largest market) actually declined 5 percent and 18 percent, respectively. At the same time the volume of Canadian end-product imports from these markets rose 23 percent and 16 percent, respectively.[4] These differences cannot be fully accounted for by a faster real growth of income in Canada. Japan's rate of real GNP growth averaged about 5.8 percent annually in 1977-78, a rate substantially above the Canadian rate of about 3 percent. For countries such as Germany the real growth of GNP was 3.2 percent annually in 1977-78. These results are consistent with the view that one must look beyond the performance of relative prices and incomes in examining the comparative trade achievements of developed countries.

A recent study covering the 1970-74 period identified Canada's relatively poor export performance for these years as being only in a small way, if at all, attributable to the fact that Canadian exports are sold primarily to one of the slower growing markets — the United States. More important was Canada's heavy reliance upon exports of crude and semi-manufactured materials, for which world markets have been expanding less rapidly than for all highly manufactured goods. Most important of all were those factors affecting the competitiveness of Canadian industry (and that lie behind the relative lack of new investment during the past decade).[5]

Merchandise imports accounted for 23.4 percent of total domestic outlays on commodities in 1966-67, 27.8 percent in 1970-71, and 31.5 percent in 1974-77.[6] Hence nearly one-third of all goods purchased by Canadians now come from abroad.

Table 19 shows Canadian trade balances, by major commodity group, between 1965 and 1978. There are surpluses in agricultural and forest products and crude and semi-processed minerals, and deficits in automobiles and especially in trade in other highly manufactured commodities — that is, Canada's surpluses generally exist

[4] Statistics Canada, *Summary of External Trade,* May, 1977 (Ottawa, 1977), December, 1978, *op. cit.,* and January, 1979 (Ottawa, 1979); Department of Finance, *Economic Review,* 1978 (Ottawa, 1978). In value terms, highly manufactured exports to Japan rose 12 percent, while those to the EEC (excluding the United Kingdom) declined 3 percent. Imports from these two areas rose a remarkable 55 percent and 45 percent, respectively.

[5] See Appendix C, where we report a few of the results from this study by James E. Powell, entitled "A Constant Market Share Analysis of Canadian Export Growth: 1970-1974," Department of Economics, University of Alberta, March, 1978.

[6] Economic Council of Canada, *op. cit.,* Table 2.1, p. 22.

TABLE 19

Canadian Trade Balances, by Major Commodity Group, 1965-78[a]
(billion dollars)

	1965-66	1970-71	1976-77	1978
	(1)	(2)	(3)	(4)
Agricultural products	1.0	.9	1.3	1.6
Forest products	2.0	2.8	6.4	8.7
Crude minerals (except energy products)	1.0	1.7	2.8	2.3
Energy products	-.2	.3	1.2	1.3
Semi-processed minerals[b]	.3	.9	.6	2.0
Automobiles and parts	-.7	.3	-1.2	-.8
Other highly manufactured goods[c]	-3.1	-4.1	-11.5	-12.8
Special transactions (trade)	-.3	-.1	-.4	-.3
	0	2.7	-.8	2.0

[a] These figures will not add up to those presented in Table 1, as Table 1 figures have been adjusted to a national accounts basis and these have not.
[b] Including all iron and steel products classified as "fabricated materials, inedible" in Canadian trade statistics.
[c] Including industrial and agricultural equipment, other transportation equipment, other equipment and tools, textiles and chemicals, and leather and rubber products.
Source: Statistics Canada, *Summary of External Trade*, December, 1978 (Ottawa, 1979).

in those commodities for which the long-run income elasticity of demand is quite low (frequently below unity). In other words, as foreign incomes expand, demand for these products expands less than in proportion to the growth in income. In contrast, Canada's deficits are in those commodities for which the income elasticity of demand is relatively high — that is, as incomes grow, demand grows more than in proportion to the income growth. Hence, if the nation continues to specialize primarily in exporting relatively unprocessed agricultural, forestry, and mineral products while importing primarily highly manufactured commodities, it can expect that, in the absence of upward shifts in the volumes and/or prices of these renewable and non-renewable resource-based exports or unless other resource exports become increasingly important (such as fish products, because of the 200-mile limit) or unless a persistently slower rate of income growth is experienced in Canada than in other developed nations, as was true vis-à-vis the United States in 1977-78 (with some resulting favorable income effects upon the Canadian trade balance with that country), Canada's merchandise trade balance will tend to deteriorate, not improve, over the longer run.

These remarks all suggest that, although there has been an improvement in Canada's trade position since the dollar began to depreciate in late 1976,[7] the structural problems in the economy, discussed in earlier chapters, are still being reflected in the characteristics of, and trends in, the nation's balance of merchandise trade.

We turn now to the other components of the Canadian balance of payments.

The Non-Merchandise and Capital Accounts

Table 20 provides a summary of Canada's balance of payments since 1956. This presentation differs from the official statistics because, consistent with the discussion of savings in Chapter 3, annual retained earnings of foreign subsidiaries in Canada are shown here as a service charge on the massive foreign investment in this country (column 6), with the offsetting entry being an increment to foreign direct investment (column 14). This procedure is widely recognized among economists as a more appropriate method of balance of payments accounting than the manner in which Statistics Canada continues to present Canadian data.[8] A number of trends and issues are highlighted by this table.

• Because of the size of retained earnings, the deficits on debt service charges and the total current account are, in fact, much larger than is usually realized. The former was $7.3 billion, and the latter $8.3 billion, in 1978.

---

[7] For example, in 1978 the volume of exports of end-product manufactures, excluding automobiles and parts, rose by about 20 percent, whereas imports of such products rose only about 7 percent; but because such exports make up only one-third of the corresponding import category, the absolute dollar deficit for trade in these products still expanded.

[8] For example, the International Monetary Fund (*Balance of Payments Manual,* 4th ed. [Washington, D.C., 1977], paragraphs 291 and 294) endorses this view. So did the Bureau of the Budget's Review Committee for Balance of Payments Statistics in *The Balance of Payments Statistics of the United States: A Review and Appraisal* (Washington, D.C.: U.S. Government Printing Office, 1965). The United States now follows this approach in its balance of payments. In principle, Statistics Canada accepts this position, and when stock dividends are declared by subsidiaries to their foreign parents, or when foreign branches in Canada (as distinguished from the more common separately incorporated subsidiary) retain their profits, the statisticians handle these in the same way as all retained earnings are handled in Table 20 — current-account payments to foreign parents are increased, as are receipts of direct investment funds in the long-term capital account.

It is of interest to note also that Statistics Canada now presents quite up-to-date preliminary estimates of the Canadian balance of international indebtedness, rather than lagging years behind in its figures as it used to. I hope that this means that Statistics Canada is preparing itself for the transition to a more appropriate balance of payments presentation.

TABLE 20

Canadian Balance of Payments, 1956-78
(million Canadian dollars)

(a) Current Account

	Merchandise Trade Balance	Non-Merchandise Trade									Current-Account Balance
		Freight and Shipping	Travel	Service Charges on Debt				Other Service Items	Net Transfers and Available Gold [b]	Total Non-Merchandise Items	
				Interest	Dividends	Retained Earnings [a]	Total				
	(1)	(2)	(3)	(4)	(5)	(6)	(7)	(8)	(9)	(10)	(11)
1956	-728	-45	-161	-90	-292	-400	-782	-89	33	-1,044	-1,772
1957	-594	-70	-162	-110	-331	-425	-866	-194	10	-1,282	-1,876
1958	-176	-59	-193	-118	-329	-235	-682	-246	-16	-1,196	-1,372
1959	-421	-105	-207	-140	-351	-350	-841	-224	-39	-1,416	-1,837
1960	-148	-91	-160	-163	-322	-280	-765	-259	-43	-1,365	-1,513
1961	173	-82	-160	-180	-371	-240	-791	-282	-26	-1,341	-1,168
1962	184	-86	-43	-194	-387	-325	-906	-315	11	-1,339	-1,155
1963	503	-85	24	-215	-415	-435	-1,065	-332	-1	-1,459	-956
1964	701	-35	-50	-251	-427	-480	-1,158	-353	-9	-1,605	-904
1965	118	-93	-49	-289	-475	-735	-1,499	-342	0	-1,983	-1,865
1966	224	-65	-60	-319	-503	-640	-1,462	-414	-25	-2,026	-1,802
1967	566	-31	423	-369	-547	-845	-1,761	-507	-34	-1,910	-1,344
1968	1,471	-40	-29	-444	-462	-810	-1,716	-601	9	-2,377	-906
1969	964	-61	-214	-489	-426	-1,045	-1,960	-600	-91	-2,926	-1,962
1970	3,052	20	-216	-503	-519	-905	-1,927	-612	-116	-2,851	201
1971	2,563	-12	-202	-535	-606	-1,380	-2,521	-765	-12	-3,512	-49
1972	1,857	-74	-234	-592	-456	-1,580	-2,628	-884	-3	-3,823	-1,966
1973	2,735	-66	-296	-656	-604	-2,370	-3,630	-1,027	22	-4,997	-2,262
1974	1,689	-224	-284	-673	-880	-2,745	-4,298	-1,215	127	-5,894	-4,205
1975	-451	-433	-727	-968	-985	-2,665	-4,618	-1,108	-85	-6,971	-7,422
1976	1,339	-148	-1,191	-1,566	-906	-2,800	-5,272	-1,336	7	-7,940	-6,601
1977	2,916	-68	-1,641	-2,457	-1,023	-2,800	-6,280	-1,709	-168	-9,866	-6,950
1978	3,468	-51	-1,719	-3,200	-1,105	-3,000	-7,305	-2,072	-606	-11,753	-8,285

(b) Capital Account and Changes in Reserves

	Capital Account								
	Net Portfolio Capital (12)	Net Direct Investment		Total Direct Investment (15)	Balance on Long-Term Capital (16)	Basic Balance on Current Account and Long-Term Capital (17)	Net Short-Term Capital (18)	Capital-Account Balance (19)	Change in Reserves [c] (20)
		Net Recorded Flows (13)	Retained Earnings [a] (14)						
1956	945	545	400	945	1,890	118	-70	1,820	48
1957	855	465	425	890	1,745	-131	26	1,771	-105
1958	763	390	235	625	1,388	16	93	1,481	109
1959	694	485	350	835	1,529	-308	297	1,826	-11
1960	309	620	280	900	1,209	-304	265	1,474	-39
1961	450	480	240	720	1,170	2	290	1,460	292
1962	288	400	325	725	1,013	-142	296	1,309	154
1963	492	145	435	580	1,072	116	29	1,101	145
1964	575	175	480	655	1,230	326	38	1,268	364
1965	423	410	735	1,145	1,568	-297	455	2,023	158
1966	443	785	640	1,425	1,868	66	-425	1,443	-361
1967	849	566	845	1,411	2,260	916	-896	1,364	20
1968	1,304	365	810	1,175	2,479	1,573	-1,223	1,256	349
1969	1,987	350	1,045	1,395	3,382	1,420	-1,355	2,027	65
1970	417	590	905	1,495	1,912	2,113	-583	1,324	1,663
1971	-31	695	1,380	2,075	2,044	1,095	-318	1,726	896
1972	1,368	220	1,580	1,800	3,168	1,202	-983	2,185	336
1973	420	-35	2,370	2,335	2,755	493	-960	1,795	-467
1974	921	-50	2,745	2,695	3,616	-589	613	4,229	24
1975	3,973	-125	2,665	2,540	6,513	909	504	7,017	-405
1976	8,724	-850	2,800	1,950	10,674	4,078	-3,551	7,123	522
1977	4,726	-380	2,800	2,420	7,146	196	-1,617	5,529	-1,421
1978	5,468	-2,015	3,000	985	6,453	-1,832	-1,467	4,986	-3,299

[a] In general, retained earnings are, on the one hand, overstated because no estimate is currently available on "inflows" of retained earnings on direct investment abroad by Canadian-owned companies. On the other hand, they are understated because no provision has been made for retained earnings attributable to foreigners holding portfolio investments of Canadian capital stock. These two

sources of bias would approximately cancel out because Canadian direct investment abroad equals about one-fifth of foreign direct investment in Canada and, after being adjusted downward for foreign interests in Canadian direct investment abroad, about one-tenth of foreign direct investment in Canada. Portfolio investments in Canadian stock by foreigners also equal about one-tenth of foreign direct investment in Canada. (See source for retained earnings below.)

[b] Includes inheritances and migrants' funds, personal institutional remittances, and withholding taxes netted out to zero.

[c] Including SDR allocations in 1970, 1971, and 1972 of $133 million, $119 million, and $117 million, respectively.

Sources: For all items except retained earnings see Statistics Canada, *Quarterly Estimates of the Canadian Balance of International Payments*, various issues. For retained earnings see Statistics Canada, *Canada's International Investment Position, 1971-1973* (Ottawa, 1977). For 1974-78, estimates were used.

• Although popular concern has been appropriately expressed about the increased cost of paying the interest charges on recent, exceptionally large debt-capital borrowings (often by provincial and municipal governments and their crown corporations), such charges — although large and rising at a disconcerting rate — are still substantially less than one-half of dividends and retained earnings combined.

• Since 1963 — with the exception of 1966 — undistributed profits have been a larger source of increased foreign control of the Canadian economy than have new capital direct investment inflows. In fact, over the 1956-78 period the former were about six times larger than the latter. (Such retained profits have risen not only in absolute terms but as a percentage of dividends paid to non-residents — from 66 percent in the first half of the 1960s to 166 percent in the early 1970s. Companies apparently have been withdrawing a much smaller proportion of their earnings from Canada, presumably because of the desire to expand here and/or to replace depreciated capital at the inflated prices of today and/or to avoid U.S. taxes on repatriated profits.)

• The deficit on "other" service items is also growing rapidly. About 20-25 percent of this deficit (amounting to $370 million in 1976, for example) could be included under service charges on Canada's international indebtedness, for it covers payments for mortgages, long-term intercompany and bank loans, real estate holdings, and earnings on short-term investments of both a bank and a non-bank nature. These particular net payments amounted to less than $100 million as recently as 1970, so their growth has been dramatic. Most of the remainder of this account is net payment for business services of all types, such as royalties, patents and associated charges, management and consultants' fees, and charges for foreign technology. Many of these net charges are therefore also the result of foreign investment — especially direct investment — in Canada.

• A large increase has occurred in the travel deficit in recent years as Canadians have progressively acquired a taste for vacationing in warmer climates in the winter and for exploring the roots of their heritage in Europe during the summer.

• The freight and shipping deficit has tended to expand spasmodically as well. Canada does not have a merchant marine, so its exports and imports by water require the services of foreign ships.

In summary, all major components of the non-merchandise portion of the current account have generally been registering growing deficits. What is more, most of these deficits may tend to swell in the future. As net capital inflows continue, net service charges of all types — interest, dividends, retained profits, and managerial and technological expenses — will follow suit. Freight and shipping costs may also grow. Net foreign travel charges may decline somewhat, provided the Canadian dollar remains well below parity with the U.S. dollar. But to some extent, the deterrent effect of the higher costs of foreign travel may be more than offset by the positive effect of the higher incomes Canadians now enjoy and their growing preference for, and ability to pay for, winter vacations in the sun. Certainly this seems to have been true for 1978.[9]

Three other comments are worth making in relation to the overall balance of payments position as portrayed in Table 20. First, observe that the balance of payments figures do not reflect any changes in inventories. It has been suggested that, in assessing the state of a nation's external accounts, alterations in its inventories of goods entering international trade should be taken into account.[10] For example, if a country were running a merchandise trade deficit but were piling up compensating large inventories of imported raw materials or other inputs to be used for future manufacturing and/or direct consumption (perhaps because of the threat of a labor strike affecting major suppliers abroad), the deficit should not be viewed with any alarm. Conversely, balanced trade, or even a surplus, accompanied by a more than compensating depletion of inventories of importables and/or exportables may require some policy changes to rectify the situation.

This observation has relevance for Canada. The trade surpluses generated annually over 17 of the 23 years shown in Table 20 have been accompanied by a steady depletion of Canadian inventories of non-renewable mineral resources. In 1977-78, when the annual merchandise trade surplus averaged $3.2 billion, crude mineral exports — including petroleum and natural gas — comprised an annual average of $7.5 billion, or 23.6 percent of all exports.[11] Viewed in this light, the Canadian balance of payments is less favorable than the numbers indicate.[12]

---

[9] Even though the average U.S.-dollar value of the Canadian dollar in 1978 was 7-8 cents less than in 1977, the tourist deficit rose by 4.8 percent. The slower rate of expansion of the deficit was a consequence of a decline in the rate of increase of tourist outlays by Canadians traveling abroad in 1978 to 10 percent from 20 percent in the previous two or three years and of an increase in the outlays by foreigners coming to Canada of 15 percent or so compared with annual increments of 6 percent in the preceding three years (see Ian MacKay and Robert Hannah, "Canada's Balance of Payments in the 1970s: A Perspective," *Bank of Canada Review,* March, 1979 [Ottawa, 1979]).

For 1979 a decline in the travel deficit has occurred, however, because of both a surge of foreigners coming to Canada and a decline in Canadians going abroad (Statistics Canada, *Daily Bulletin,* November 22, 1979).

[10] C. P. Kindleberger, "Measuring Equilibrium in the Balance of Payments," *Journal of Political Economy,* November-December, 1969, pp. 873-91.

[11] If semi-processed Canadian minerals were also included, the figures would be even larger.

[12] There are, of course, a host of questions that could be raised at this juncture regarding the valuation of the resources exported (some part of their export value is the

Second, Canada's massive international borrowing in recent years (Canada has been the world's largest long-term borrower the past few years) has resulted in the country's net international indebtedness, at book value, growing to over $65 billion, or about $2,700 per capita. Canada thus is the leading debtor in the industrialized world.[13] (If market values were employed for foreign direct investment in Canada, the numbers would be even larger.)

Note also that Canada's cumulative net non-merchandise deficit with the United States from 1946 to 1978, excluding retained earnings, amounted to $44 billion. If undistributed earnings are included, another $23 billion is involved, giving a total of $67 billion over the 32-year period. If the cumulative deficit on merchandise trade is introduced, the figure becomes about $71 billion.

Third, a tendency exists on the part of some economists to view Canada's current-account deficits with complacency. One reason for this may be a belief in the "balance-of-payments-stages-of-growth" theory,[14] according to which countries can be expected to move from the young debtor stage, where current-account payments exceed receipts and are balanced, or more than balanced, by long-term capital inflows — the situation that Canada has been in for all the years of its existence, with a few exceptions such as in the 1930s and during and shortly after World War II — to the adult debtor stage, where the current account is balanced, and then on to the mature debtor and young creditor stages, where net repayments begin and net lending follows.

That the United States moved from the young debtor to the young creditor stage in the short period of World War I is sometimes cited as evidence that this process occurs and that Canada too will follow this pattern in due course. However, the circumstances of the

---

return on the capital and payments to labor used in their exploitation); the size of remaining reserves of non-replaceable resources; the accessibility and quality of these reserves relative to other sources in the world and to future world prices; and changing market demand for various minerals as technology changes, substitutes are developed, more recycling occurs, and so on. However, these issues would require another paper with quite a different focus. It is sufficient here to observe that depletion of raw materials inventories is an issue that should be taken into account when assessing Canada's balance of payments situation.

[13] If we consider just long-term debt as a percentage of GNP, Canada, with a ratio of about 22 percent, is again the leader among industrialized nations and more in line with developing nations such as Taiwan, Peru, and Mexico (R. Sultan, "Energy Finance," paper presented to The Conference Board in Canada's Fourth Canadian Financial Conference, Montreal, June 28-29, 1977).

[14] Early editions (for example, the revised edition) of C. P. Kindleberger's well-known textbook, *International Economics* (Homewood, Ill.: Richard Irwin, 1958), emphasized this balance of payments stages-of-development theory. Later editions dropped it altogether. Simon Kuznets ("International Differences in Capital Formation and Financing," in *Capital Formation and Economic Growth* [Princeton: Princeton University Press, 1955]) erroneously held the view that nations such as Canada and Australia were shifting from net debtor to net creditor positions internationally.

TABLE 21

**Measures of the Importance of Net Foreign Investment[a]
to the Canadian Economy, 1956-78**
(percentages)

	Current-Account Deficit (Net Foreign Investment) As Percentage of		Net Long-Term Capital Inflows As Percentage of Gross Investment (Excluding Residential Construction)[c]	Net Debt/Service Ratio (Interest, Dividends, and Retained Earnings As Percentage of Merchandise Exports)
	GNP[b]	Gross Investment (Excluding Residential Construction)[c]		
	(1)	(2)	(3)	(4)
1956-57	5.5	25.7	25.6	16.9
1960-61	3.4	19.0	16.8	13.8
1965-66	3.2	14.5	13.5	15.7
1970-71	2.3	2.3	10.8	12.8
1975-76	4.3	23.5	26.4	14.0
1977-78	3.4	20.5	18.3	14.0

[a]Including retained earnings of foreign corporations.
[b]GNP and the rest of the national accounts actually should be adjusted to exclude retained profits of foreign-owned firms. Accordingly, the percentages in this column for recent years — especially 1975-76 — would be a little higher than shown. I am grateful to T. L. Powrie for a comment that suggested this point.
[c]Gross investment, rather than net investment, was used because capital consumption allowances were not available separately for residential construction. Hence any net figures employed would be, in reality, neither gross nor net. (Not surprisingly, perhaps, the trends are, nevertheless, very similar when the gross figures are adjusted for total capital consumption allowances.)

Residential construction was excluded because of its normally very heavy reliance on domestic capital sources and because it is, essentially, for producing nontradables. (Once again, however, calculations including residential construction produce a pattern comparable to the one reported in Table 2.) Changes in non-farm inventories were also included.

Sources: Statistics Canada, *Quarterly Estimates of the Canadian Balance of International Payments*, various issues; Bank of Canada, *Bank of Canada Review* (Ottawa, various issues).

U.S. transformation were obviously exceptional because that country was able to generate large trade balances from selling to both sides during much of the war. In addition, at that time most U.S. foreign indebtedness was in the form of debt capital, which is not self-expanding by means of undistributed profits when prosperity occurs, as is so much of the investment today in Canada.

There is nothing automatic or inexorable, however, about a nation being transformed from a young debtor into a mature debtor and eventually into a young creditor. From the mid-1950s until the end of the 1960s, Canada's net indebtedness rose steadily. Borrowing as a percentage of GNP or of gross investment and service costs as a percentage of merchandise exports seemed to be declining. But by the mid-1970s these magnitudes were once again back to somewhere near their levels of the 1950s (see Table 21). In other words, whether Canada ever begins to repay its net international indebtedness will depend not upon some automatic adjustment mechanism of economics but upon the choices made by individuals and the various interest groups in the economy and upon the policies followed by federal and provincial governments as well as by Canada's trading partners, especially the United States.

These comments lead us to a second common reason for complacency with huge current-account deficits. There is a strong tendency in Canada to look only at the "overall balance" — that is, the balance on current account and long-term capital accounts taken together. According to this perspective, if long-term capital inflows are equal, or even more than equal, to the current-account deficit, then the international accounts are deemed in balance. Hence questions may never be asked as to whether long-term capital inflows are necessary and/or desirable. Yet enough has been said already in this monograph to suggest that long-term capital inflows are not always an unmitigated blessing.[15] Moreover, if such inflows are used simply to finance additional domestic consumption rather than either directly to expand investment or to free employed resources from producing consumer goods so that such resources can be used to produce new capital goods, the nation is clearly living beyond its means. We shall return to questions of this sort in Chapter 8.

Concluding Remarks

Although Canada's merchandise trade account has been improving — particularly since the Canadian dollar again fell below parity with the U.S. dollar and while U.S. output growth has been reasonably strong — it has not kept pace with the expansion of the deficits on other items in the current account. Consequently, Canada's long-term indebtedness continues to grow, and at an increasing rate in current dollars. Moreover, Canadian trade surpluses are in crude and semi-processed products, for which world demand generally does not grow as rapidly as for highly manufactured goods. This fact, coupled with significant structural problems in Canadian manufacturing and the expected heavy investment required for energy resource development, suggests that — in the absence of significant changes in either domestic policies or the external environment, or both — current-account deficits, and hence foreign capital inflows, of considerable magnitude will continue well into the future.

---

[15] See, for example, the sections entitled "Foreign Ownership" and "Economies of Scale" in Chapter 4 and the sections entitled "Economic Rents and Foreign Ownership" and "Employment Issues" in Chapter 5.

7

Summary

In the 1980s the Canadian labor force is expected to expand no more than 2 percent annually (and possibly at a much lower rate). This rate is well below the average over the 1970s, and the main reasons are that the rate of growth of those of labor force age is dropping following the reduction in birth rates during the 1960s and into the 1970s; net immigration is expected to be less than it has been; and the growth of female labor-force-participation rates is likely to taper off. Consequently, even though dependency ratios may continue to decline modestly over the next 10-15 years, the expanding proportion of the population in the older age categories — with attendant increases in health care costs — will mean that little improvement in per capita incomes can be expected from any additional reduction in dependency ratios as the labor force expands. Also, the average time each worker is on the job will continue to diminish as weekly hours decrease and the number of paid holidays and the length of vacations are increased. Unemployment is anticipated to remain at levels well above those experienced, on average, in the 1960s — or "discouraged" workers may drop out of the labor force entirely.

Therefore, growth in per capita incomes will have to come primarily from improvements in labor productivity. In past years some labor productivity improvement has resulted from increased education levels among new workers (although this may have been offset, in part, by their lack of on-the-job training and experience) and from shifts of workers from relatively low-productivity sectors — such as agriculture — to higher-productivity sectors; from provinces with relatively low productivity to provinces with higher productivity; and from rural areas to urban centers. In the future some quality improvements should be possible from the growing on-the-job experience of the young people and women who have joined the work force in the 1970s, but it is unlikely that a continuation of structural shifts of the types just mentioned can again produce the magnitudes of productivity increase that have occurred over the past two decades or so.

The role of the physical capital with which labor has to work thus warrants attention. A rough positive relationship occurs between capital/labor ratios and output per employee, but alterations in such ratios do not produce easily identifiable alterations in productivity. In the short run, for example, changes in the degree of capacity utilization alone explain almost perfectly observed variations in output per employee. Unused capacity reduces productivity. In the longer run other forces relating to the organization of production (scale, length of production run, and so forth), the technology employed, the capability of management, and changing external conditions all play a role. Hence it is not only a matter of increasing capital/labor ratios in order to improve labor productivity and competitiveness of industry — although higher capital/labor ratios certainly are the trend in many sectors, especially in mining and energy production in all its forms. Moreover, even though developments such as the drop in corporate ratios of internal to external financing, of share capital to debt borrowing, and of long-term to short-term indebtedness are worth mentioning, the variety of apparently operational formulas according to which companies in divergent industries and countries can function suggest that these are not the crucial issues. Of more importance are questions relating to the aggregate supply of real savings available; the degree to which foreign sources of funds need to be, or should be, relied upon; whether appropriate incentives exist for firms to invest in Canada and/or take such efficiency-improving steps as may be necessary to enhance Canadian productivity and ability to compete in domestic and foreign markets; and whether federal and provincial government policies will be supportive of the changes that are necessary.

We have examined the altering world environment in relation to Canada's traditional industrial structure, its domestic employment situation, and its international trade patterns. We noted, on the one hand, the desire of developing nations to share more fully in the world's material riches by taking over a larger share of its production of labor-intensive and mass-produced assembly-line products, including the processing of tropical goods and the mining and processing of minerals; by appropriating and using advanced technology where feasible; and by gaining favored access to the markets of the West. On the other hand, it was noted that there is an increasing emphasis among Western nations on high-technology exports (and sustained protectionism in one form or another, even though the Tokyo Round of GATT negotiations has produced some reductions in tariffs) in order to pay for, or to restrain, additional imports of the above products from the poor countries as well as high-priced energy supplies from the OPEC nations. Canada is caught between these two sets of forces and is somewhat ill-equipped in its present state of disarray to cope effectively with either of them. Internal fragmentation and inefficiency of manufacturing, with provincial protectionism contributing to the sector's problem; a lack of advanced native technology and, not infrequently, of world marketing rights on technology from abroad; a relative absence of worldwide sales agencies by many companies, owing either to a dirth of aggressiveness or to reliance upon foreign parents and affiliates to handle foreign sales; undue emphasis upon labor-intensive products and processes in domestic manufacturing; diminished comparative advantage in a variety of crude mineral resources and in the processing thereof; domestic protectionism of much non-grain agricultural production, which decreases, if anything, the industry's ability to compete in world markets — all these factors contribute to this unpreparedness.

Canada has found it difficult to sustain, let alone expand, its markets in developed countries (other than the United States, where trade has been increasingly concentrated and with which there are many corporate ties) and to take advantage of markets opening up in developing countries as the latter expand their sales to the West (although Canadian sales to OPEC countries have grown).[1] Moreover, Canada depends for a large proportion of export receipts upon raw and semi-fabricated materials, for which world demand tends to grow less rapidly than income, while its imports are primarily of highly manufactured goods, the demand for which grows faster, relative to income, than for crude and semi-processed materials. Substantial new gains in the merchandise trade account may therefore not be easily forthcoming — especially with more intense competition from new mineral- and other resource-producing nations entering world trade.

The depreciation of the Canadian dollar in 1977-78 (to about U.S.$0.85) helped Canadian industry compete with imports, particularly where the source of any lack of competitiveness was internal inflationary pressures. However, if Canadians attempt to offset the loss of purchasing power stemming from the depreciation by a new round of excessive wage and salary demands, the benefit of the depreciation will soon be lost and the process will have to repeat itself.[2] More important, a number of the structural and other problems outlined — such as those associated with low-skill-level, labor-intensive production; the lack of advanced technology; inadequate financial support to bring new ideas to the marketplace after the initial R & D is completed; provincial protectionism; industrial fragmentation; and insufficient vision and initiative — will not be readily resolved simply by a depreciation of the dollar, even if the beneficial effects upon competitiveness are not eroded by domestic wage and price inflation. Internal reorganization and other changes will

---

[1] In their projections for the *Fourteenth Annual Review* (Ottawa, 1977), the Economic Council of Canada assumed that rapid increases in sales to OPEC countries would continue. It is not clear whether this assumption was continued in their models for the *Fifteenth Annual Review* (Ottawa, 1978).

[2] The Ontario Economic Council, in its projections to 1987, clearly allows for this possibility (J. Sawyer, D. Dungan, and J. W. Winder, *The Ontario Economy: 1978-1987* [Toronto: Ontario Economic Council, 1978], p. 35).

still be required in order to achieve productivity gains anywhere near those attained in the past few decades and to develop a correspondingly improved capability to compete in world markets. Such alterations will also be useful in helping to counter, if possible, the adverse effects upon national productivity of both escalating energy costs and the need to devote more resources to enlarge high-cost domestic energy production.

The Economic Council's nine different projections of productivity growth to 1986 average 1.9 percent annually for output per man-hour and 1.5 percent annually for output per employed person.[3] These estimates are substantially below the average productivity growth over the past 30 years.[4] Judging from the discussion in preceding chapters, these estimates do not appear unduly low. Indeed, they could turn out to be on the generous side.

Finally, continuing balance of payments current-account deficits are anticipated, so that dependence upon large capital inflows is expected to be a persistent part of the Canadian economic scene.

This provides us with a general picture of the Canadian economy at the end of the 1970s. Having emerged from several decades of great prosperity, Canada now faces the prospect of continuing lower rates of growth of productivity, output, and income per capita, partially because alternate sources of supply are becoming more competitive in products where Canada has traditionally had some trade advantage, partially because Canada itself seems to have failed to keep up with the world pace of technological change and structural reorganization of production, and partially because imposed upon these circumstances is the specter of spiraling energy costs, international unemployment, and slower world economic growth in general, coupled with sustained, widespread inflation.

It is natural, therefore, to ask, Where do we go from here? There are no easy answers. What appears obvious, however, is that a "life-as-usual" approach, on the grounds that in the long run everything is bound to work out, is not an adequate response to the current and future environment. It is far beyond the scope of this monograph to attempt any detailed prescriptions for change. Still, it may not be inappropriate to sketch out several broad policy areas that warrant consideration. These form the substance of Chapter 8.

[3] R. Preston, T. Schweitzer, and J. Fortin, *Fifteenth Annual Review: Statistical Documentation* (Ottawa: Economic Council of Canada, 1978). In the Economic Council of Canada's *Sixteenth Annual Review*, average productivity growth for 1980-85 for the five scenarios chosen for analysis is projected to be 1.56 percent annually; it is not stated whether this is output per man-hour or per employed person (Economic Council of Canada, *Sixteenth Annual Review: Two Cheers for the Eighties* [Ottawa, 1979], Appendix Table 2).

[4] See Table 1 and Statistics Canada, *Aggregate Productivity Measures, 1946-1976* (Ottawa, 1978), Table 3, which shows that annual increases in output per person and output per man-hour in 1948-73 averaged 3.0 percent and 3.5 percent, respectively.

III

POLICY CONSIDERATIONS

8

Key Policy Issues

Introduction

Canada is part of the international community, and — as we have seen in earlier chapters — what happens in that community is of fundamental importance for Canadian competitiveness and development. Even so, it does not follow that Canada's role must always be one of passive reliance upon forces from abroad. In fact, if one single conclusion had to be drawn from the preceding chapters, it should be that Canada must not simply look to factors and forces beyond its own boundaries to improve its internal lot. As noted in the introduction to Part II of this paper, Canada has, by international standards, a fairly well-educated labor force and a structure within which the necessary additional training and retraining programs could be developed. It also has, compared to most wealthy nations, a high ratio of replaceable and non-replaceable natural resources to population. These human and natural resources are linked by advanced transportation and communications systems. So the question might be asked, To what extent are Canadians limited by their own lack of imagination and initiative and by an unwillingness to adapt quickly enough to changing circumstances?

In the sections that follow, three broad suggestions are put forward regarding measures that Canada might take to strengthen its economic performance and to contribute simultaneously to an improved world economic environment. They relate to the internal restructuring of industry; to the possibility of greater tied aid to developing countries; and to the merits of maintaining a relatively low value for the Canadian dollar while moving toward an objective of a balanced current account.

It must be emphasized that these suggestions are not meant to be a comprehensive prescription for Canada's economic malaise. Nor has an attempt been made to delineate and weigh every possible aspect and implication of these recommendations. Rather they are submitted for discussion in the hope that others will be stimulated to examine them. They tend to be unconventional, but perhaps we have reached a point where unconventional approaches have some merit.

The Restructuring of Canadian Industry

A commonly held view is that, regardless of any success of the Tokyo Round of GATT negotiations, a free-trade arrangement with the United States is highly desirable, if not essential, for the restructuring of Canadian industry. However, one must have many reservations about proceeding, at this time, with such Canadian-U.S. negotiations, and the reader is referred to Appendix D for a review of the author's reservations.

The position taken in what follows is that Canada has another option. This option will require new initiatives — at a minimum, initiatives that have already been taken in isolated instances will have to become part of a more general policy.

The essence of the idea is that Canada should insist upon a reorganization and rationalization of its manufacturing sector prior to, and as a prerequisite of, any free-trade arrangement. This does not exclude free trade as an eventual policy move. It simply means that Canada should prepare itself much better internally first. This position is consistent with the findings of recent research that a nation should look initially not to exports as the main source of domestic industrial health — as the Canadian-U.S. free-trade argument tends to suggest — but rather to "homespun growth," which in turn will have a spillover effect on foreign markets.[1]

This strategy has a variety of aspects. First, where the various plants in a national, regional, or local industry are each producing too many lines to achieve the possible economies of scale, then each would have to reduce the variety of its output and lengthen its runs. It would be difficult to persuade a company to specialize in a single product line at the risk of suffering a declining demand for this line, while another firm, specializing in a different product line, enjoyed increasing sales. Therefore, large new corporations would have to be formed, each in control of the number of specialized plants necessary for a full range of lines to be produced. They would produce commodities in sufficient volume to be competitive with the rest of the world.[2] (Canada would, of course, still have to move increasingly

---

[1] See John Cornwall, *Modern Capitalism: Its Growth and Transformation* (London: Martin Robertson, 1977), pp. 193-94. Cornwall finds that "The case of Japan, the most dynamic economy by far in the postwar period, illustrates these views. In a country assigned the highest marks for the quality of its entrepreneurship, this latter group operated with an aim to develop domestic and foreign markets. But even in this case, *growth would have to be characterized as predominantly homespun.* Thus, the analysis comes down to the rather undramatic conclusion that, *while there is a spillover from domestic markets to foreign markets and vice versa, in some long-run sense, at least, it is the former spillover that predominates*" (emphasis added).

[2] Note that amendments to the proposed Competition Act — Bill C-42 — would not preclude mergers where their purpose was to enhance efficiency (see D. P. DeMelto, "The Role of Competition Policy in the Adaptation of Canadian Industry to Change," paper presented to the Economic Council of Canada's Conference on Industrial Adaptation, Montreal, June 27-28, 1977).

away from specialization in labor-intensive commodities, for these are clearly the domain of the developing countries.)

The major argument usually made against such a policy is that U.S. subsidiaries, which form an important segment of many Canadian industries, might be unwilling to cooperate in joint ventures of the type suggested, for fear of violating U.S. anti-trust laws. Too much is made of this possibility. U.S. parents would not be asked to merge. New companies would be established in Canada, and foreign subsidiaries could hold shares in them. There are already many instances of U.S. subsidiaries participating in joint ventures abroad — with one another, with foreign firms, and with governments. We have examples in Canada, such as Syncrude with respect to the oil sands and the new appliance-manufacturing firm, Camco, created with the government's blessing. If some U.S. firms did not wish to participate, they would have the option of withdrawing from the Canadian market. Their withdrawal would mean less U.S. ownership of Canadian industry, which would be consistent with the recommendation to be made subsequently in this chapter of reducing reliance upon foreign capital inflows. Canada is a sovereign country and, as such, is entitled to encourage such arrangements as it believes desirable. If it cannot do so, then the degree of U.S. influence on the Canadian economy has clearly already gone too far.

This brings us to another important part of this strategy, at least in its initial stages. The author is far from being in favor of general government ownership and control of industry; but given the unfavorable position Canada has, through neglect, worked itself into, it appears that government participation might well be essential in a number of, although not all, instances if the new companies were not to become totally controlled by foreign parent firms whose interests may not be those of the Canadian economy. Ontario Hydro was originally formed to prevent this sector from falling under foreign control. Also, the failure of industrial and other government policies to stimulate an adequate technological base within private industry in this country and massive control of technology abroad suggest that government participation may be the only way to develop a distinctive technology in selected sectors. Canadians need only ask themselves, Would Canada have an independent nuclear technology today if a hands-off government policy had been followed and development left to the private sector? Would Canada now have a thriving aircraft industry if the federal government had not stepped in to take over Canadair and De Haviland? Perhaps few people recall that Swiss eminence in watchmaking stems from initial government sponsorship of a firm making the movements.

A third important aspect of this strategy would be that the provincial governments would have to cease their parochial protectionism, whereby firms within their respective boundaries are given preference over firms in other provinces. Canadians cannot afford, and should not expect, to have a plant producing each commodity group in every province or region — except where the province or region is large enough or specialized enough, or isolated enough by transportation costs, that local production can compete effectively with production from elsewhere. As noted in Appendix D, there are more products for which small specialized plants can be competitive than was once thought, but where this is not true, provincial protectionism leads only to an increasingly fragmented and inefficient manufacturing sector.

This argument can be put more strongly: any policy to rationalize Canada's manufacturing sector is doomed to failure unless the nation comes to grips with provincial protectionism. This will have to involve some give and take. For example, freight rate structures might have to be altered so as not to unduly favor one location in Canada over another. Provincial regulations that do not recognize the qualifications of skilled labor and professionals from other provinces — which at present hinder the free interprovincial flow of labor — would have to be changed. Provincial and federal marketing boards and other interventions in the agricultural sector would not be permitted to encourage inefficiency and to reduce international competitiveness. In short, the provinces and regions would have to learn to cooperate with one another much more. And where government participation in industry was found to be desirable, the provinces could be involved too, provided they did not use their participation to induce the location of inefficient-sized plants within their borders.

Three arguments raised against this strategy are

- inefficiencies resulting from government involvement in decision-making regarding the location of plants, the firms and industries selected for support, and so on;
- the possibility of consumers having to put up with less choice;
- the possibility that continuing protection will perpetuate inefficiency or at least permit monopoly profits.[3]

The first of these is considered the most important. Some argue that the initial elimination of tariff restrictions would be preferable because the "market" would then decide which firms would survive and which takeovers and mergers would occur without any need for government to get into the act. This is an oversimplification. Government adjustment assistance to industries, firms, and workers is an integral part of any move to free trade. Government must still decide which industries should be encouraged and which discouraged, which firms within an industry should be given assistance, whether the assistance should be allocated in part according to regional development or employment objectives, and so on. Provinces

---

[3] This discussion draws, in part, upon Myron Gordon, "A World Scale National Corporation Strategy," *Canadian Public Policy* 4 (Winter, 1978): 46-56.

would still compete with one another for industry. It is, therefore, clearly *not* a case of government having to "pick the winners" under a domestic pre-free-trade rationalization program and letting the market "pick the winners" in a free-trade agreement. Government actions would be of vital importance in both cases.

One could argue that, under free trade, government's role might be even more complicated because there would be the need to reconcile domestic interests with the diverse, vested interests of three levels of U.S. government and U.S. parent firms. With all these inputs into the decision-making process, the likelihood that the outcome would be to Canada's long-run benefit is quite possibly *less* under an initial free-trade agreement than if Canada pursued its own internal rationalization plans in line with its long-run objectives before considering free trade in general.

The second reservation about a policy of domestic rationalization is that the choice of consumers would be reduced. This is not important, for a number of reasons. First, such a program does not mean that fewer lines are produced in total, but only that each plant is more specialized. There would still be a wide range of lines available, but not from one plant. Second, if this reduced-choice argument means that there would be fewer brands in Canada, even though a full product range might be available from brands that were produced, it is still not valid. Proponents of free trade generally argue that, because domestic producers are inefficient, they price up to the foreign price plus the tariff. If this is correct, it follows that any brand that was discontinued in Canada because of the rationalization program could still be imported at roughly the same price to consumers that they were paying when buying it from inefficient domestic subsidiaries. It would appear *relatively* more expensive because the prices of rationalized domestic production of other brands, or new brands, would be lower, but consumer choice has essentially not been narrowed. In due course, if free trade were negotiated, even this modest difference would be eliminated.

Increasing the wide choice of brands and options is not a costless benefit. The information costs of determining which brand to acquire rise; and if information is not readily available to consumers, a wider choice may lead only to bewilderment, confusion, unease, and dissatisfaction, not greater consumer benefits.

Finally, psychology tells us that, even if the three preceding counterarguments were not correct, the benefit to consumers of a wider choice is fleeting. Once it comes to be accepted and normal, the satisfaction, joy, or pleasure therefrom disappears. Similarly, choice can be reduced; and although there may be some initial displeasure, adjustment to it soon occurs, and the narrower choice is no longer important to the individual.[4]

---

[4] See Tibor Scitovsky, *The Joyless Economy: An Inquiry into Human Satisfaction and Consumer Dissatisfaction* (Toronto: Oxford University Press, 1976), especially Chap. 4.

The third argument against a policy of internal rationalization before adopting free trade is that maintaining protection permits inefficiency to persist or monopoly profits to be gained by the firms rationalizing. This need not be so. Firms would know that free trade was the eventual objective. Hence it would be in their interest to take the opportunity to rationalize among themselves along the lines suggested, prior to any such agreement being negotiated. Once the rationalization was complete, in the normal situation where several firms — newly formed or restructured — were operating, competition among them and laws against collusion would provide consumer protection until trade liberalization was complete. Even in those rare instances — such as, perhaps, in the cases of refrigerators and cigarettes — where the domestic market, under existing technology, may support only one firm, the effort necessary to prevent supernormal profits or rates of return until free trade occurred would not be all that great. Experience with the regulation of public utilities could be applied to such situations.

Those who frown upon the policies suggested here may argue that Canada cannot hope to be a technological leader in all fields and must continue to rely on foreign countries for large amounts of technology. This is true, but does Canada have to rely on them to the extent it does? Are there not areas within many industries where Canada can increasingly specialize and develop technological expertise? In this regard it is quite wrong to assume that a firm has to be a huge transnational in order to have advanced technology. The evidence suggests that small and medium-sized firms frequently have better records of developing new products and processes than do transnationals.[5]

Technology, and not just scale, is often the key to foreign sales. To put it another way, if manufacturing is the main engine of growth, technology is the fuel for that engine. Canada cannot hope to build a competitive modern manufacturing industry without it.

An area closely connected with R & D which must receive more attention if the option outlined here were to be pursued is that of adequate financing of, and support for, new ideas and products. The record of Canadian ideas that have gone abroad for development because of a lack of financial support from Canada's powerful banks and other financial institutions, or from government, is rather shocking.[6] Canada has not maintained the close liaison among banks, industry, and government development policy that has existed in nations like Japan and Germany, perhaps because of some combination of governmental, industrial, or financial timidity, lack

---

[5] See J. Jewkes et al., The Sources of Innovation, 2nd ed. (New York: Norton, 1969).
[6] J. J. Brown (Ideas in Exile: A History of Canadian Invention [Toronto: McClelland and Stewart, 1967]) provides an excellent, although somewhat disheartening, record of this process.

of imagination, or deep conservatism or perhaps simply because the nation in general is obsessed with the idea that the only aspect of banking that it should be concerned about is the rate of growth of the money supply. Whatever the reason, much room for improvement exists in the matter of support for new technology. Canadians should not worry if there are a few failures. Employing people, or assisting business to employ people, for what, on occasion, turns out to be a failure is not as wasteful as giving people unemployment or welfare payments, because much that is valuable can be learned from failures. The main danger to guard against is permitting government financing to be channeled into the hands of promoters (domestic or foreign) of ill-conceived schemes, as has occurred too frequently in this country.

This concept of more government support for business needs emphasis. Nearly everyone endorses the idea that governments should adopt policies to achieve full employment. However, there is increasing concern lest governments simply add more people to their own payrolls, a policy that does not result in the production of marketable goods and services for the rest of society. The more effective alternative is government support for output-expanding investment. This brings us to the question of the most productive form of such support.

There needs to be a continuation and expansion of the types of financial and other assistance for small business that have been developed in Canada over the past two years or so.[7] Such businesses have greater difficulty in meeting capital needs from either internally generated funds or share issuance than do larger, well-established firms. The merchant banking approach of the 1977 federal Enterprise Development Program (EDP) is an example of the type of financial help that can be made available.[8] But assistance cannot be limited to financial support. Measures to stimulate and support improvements in managerial skills and productivity (as is occurring in Japan)[9] must also be a permanent part of any program to help smaller entrepreneurs, as must assistance in enabling individuals and firms with new ideas to bring them to the marketable stage.

Finally, Canada's policies must be geared to maximizing the benefits from its natural resources, especially its non-replenishable resources. Government will have to ensure that, as much as possible, economic rents are extracted for Canadians, while not discouraging

---

[7] For a brief review of the position of small businesses in Canada, see Canadian Imperial Bank of Commerce, "Small Business in Canada," *Commercial Letter* 2 (1978), and Minister of State for Small Business, *Small Business in Canada: Perspectives* (Ottawa, 1978).

[8] *Ibid.*

[9] See Rein Peterson, *Small Business: Building a Balanced Economy* (Erin, Ontario: Press Porcepic, 1977), Chap. 2.

desired resource development. As noted in Chapter 5,[10] the appropriation of economic rents is easier, the more an industry is domestically owned and controlled and the more that processing is undertaken within the country. Consequently, the types of Canadian takeovers — such as those of Texasgulf by the Canada Development Corporation and Husky Oil by Alberta Gas Trunk Line — occurring in recent years are of considerable merit from this perspective.

Furthermore, Canada's options must be kept open to include state trading or participation in cartels should such alternatives be found necessary. No one should be put off by the thought of state trading, for that is what is already necessary in dealing with Communist, and some Latin American, countries. In a world where both transnational corporations and industrial countries are attempting to control the prices of raw materials for their own benefit, there is no reason to think that the long-run interests of Canada as a supplying country will be protected without positive action on Canada's part. The economic theory of second-best tells us that, where there exist departures from perfect competition in the system, they are likely to be necessary throughout the economic system if welfare is to be maximized.[11]

In short, the approach outlined here requires more cooperation among the various sectors and provinces of the country than has normally occurred, and a willingness to accept, where necessary, short-run costs in order to achieve long-run benefits. Aggressive entrepreneurship and managerial talent will be essential if the rationalization and restructuring of industry are to proceed effectively and efficiently; if new technology is to be developed, or acquired, and successfully introduced; and if new markets are to be sought out and old markets expanded. In turn, governments must provide the environment that both stimulates and rewards entrepreneurial-managerial initiatives.

Such a policy would result in a stronger domestic industry that would have greater Canadian participation and ownership and would be better prepared to survive, and benefit from, any subsequent free-trade negotiations.

Aid to Developing Countries[12]

Developing nations continue to require financial assistance to enable them to import machinery, equipment, and other products necessary for their economic advance. Yet the level of such aid given

---

[10] See the section entitled "Economic Rents and Foreign Ownership."

[11] For a good review of the theory, see Akira Takayama, *International Trade* (Toronto: Holt, Rinehart and Wilson, 1972), pp. 472-92.

[12] This section has benefited from discussions with Professor G. L. Helleiner of the University of Toronto, but he should not be held in any way responsible for the final argument or its format.

by the rich nations remains about one-third to one-half of one percent of their GNP.

Therefore, a second policy that Canada might adopt, in association with its own development plans, would be to provide much more aid to poor nations. The approach might be as follows: In the beginning, a few nations could be selected from among the group of poorest countries. The criteria of selection would have to include these nations' willingness to avoid devoting resources simply to such imports as luxury goods and armaments. Beyond that, the aid would be in the form of program grants, not grants or loans for specific projects. By providing grants rather than low-interest loans, Canada would avoid adding to the already onerous debt burden of the poor countries,[13] and it would avoid problems that may arise with other lending nations when export credits are granted at interest rates below internationally agreed levels. Program grants, rather than project grants, would give recipient countries greater flexibility in developing their plans and requirements. If desired, Canadian agencies, or perhaps agencies such as the International Bank for Reconstruction and Development (IBRD) and its affiliates, might assist in developing the programs.

Canada should provide the funds on a 100 percent tied basis — that is, all aid provided would have to be spent on products from Canada — although manufacturers in Canada would be able to import components, specialized equipment, and so forth, as required to complete their production commitments.

A popular argument is that tied aid is inefficient because the recipient country might meet its needs more cheaply — perhaps as much as 20 percent more cheaply — if it were able to shop around among nations.[14] But this argument ignores the point that, if the choice a developing country has is between tied aid and no aid, tied aid involving a grant and therefore no repayment obligations is certainly superior. It could clearly obtain much more financial assistance than Canada might otherwise consider it possible to provide, and there would still be competition among suppliers in Canada for foreign sales, which would contribute to keeping prices competitive.

The advantage to Canada of such a strategy would be more markets for Canadian-made products. This would be consistent with domestic rationalization plans to increase length of runs, achieve other economies of plant or firm scale, and improve productivity. Domestic employment and income would be created too. The higher incomes would naturally mean additional imports of other products from Canada's trading partners. Hence the Canadian dollar would

[13]North-South Institute, *Third World Deficits and the Debt Crisis* (Ottawa, 1977).

[14]North-South Institute, *North-South Encounter: The Third World and Canadian Performance* (Ottawa, 1977), pp. 125-28.

tend to depreciate somewhat, thereby stimulating additional exports, domestic production, and employment.

By giving large grants to LDCs (while simultaneously pursuing a policy of internal restructuring), Canada would be setting an example to the rest of the world of providing greater assistance (relative to national income) to LDCs than is presently forthcoming. The result might well be that other nations would adopt similar policies and the LDCs would accordingly be helped much more, right across the board, than they have been to date. Such assistance might well help diffuse the LDCs' growing resentment and bitterness that the rich nations as a group have failed to keep their promises of greater developmental assistance. The current dissatisfaction of the LDCs with the minimal benefits to them from the Tokyo Round is but one example of these feelings. No one would want to see the resentment escalate and become more virulent, as could occur with the dissemination of nuclear installations and the potential for adapting these to other than peaceful uses — notwithstanding attempted safeguards on sales of nuclear plants.[15]

A Balance of Payments and Exchange Rate Strategy

We observed earlier that the depreciation of the Canadian dollar since late 1976 was necessary to restore Canadian competitiveness vis-à-vis the United States. Balance of payments figures for the first quarter of 1979, however, suggest that the road to removing the current-account deficit will not be easy. The seasonally adjusted surplus on merchandise trade for this period actually registered a 50 percent decline from a year earlier. Simultaneously, the value of imports — especially of highly manufactured products such as machinery and equipment — rose rapidly, so that imports outpaced exports.[16]

It would be satisfying to be able to recommend a sharp reduction in long-term borrowing abroad so that the Canadian dollar could be allowed to depreciate even more, thereby making domestic industry more competitive. Indeed, basic economic analysis suggests that, when there are unemployed resources of labor and capital, it is generally unnecessary to rely on foreign sources of funds for the medium and longer run and that there may even be a variety of net adverse effects from doing so — such as burdening the nation with foreign indebtedness that it need not have had if adequate domestic financing had been available.[17]

---

[15] See Lincoln P. Bloomfield, "Nuclear Spread and World Order," *Foreign Affairs* 53 (July, 1975): 743-55.

[16] Statistics Canada, *Daily Bulletin*, June 7, 1979.

[17] For a discussion of this and associated topics, see B. W. Wilkinson, "Long Term Capital Inflows and Balance of Payments Policy," in Canada Studies Foundation, *The Walter L. Gordon Lecture Series, 1979*, Vol. 2, *An Economic Strategy for Canada* (Toronto, 1980).

However, it may be argued that the immediate situation is somewhat irregular in that, although substantial reserves of unemployed labor are available, industry — manufacturing at least — is operating at fairly close to capacity.[18] Hence not much room may exist for *immediately* supplying additional exports or import-substituting processed goods even if capital inflows were discouraged greatly and the Canadian dollar were thereby permitted to depreciate to a substantially lower level. The result might be additional inflationary pressures. Some more modest capital inflows may be seen, therefore, as necessary *in the short run* in order to buy time and permit capacity to be enlarged. From this perspective, capital inflows have to be sustained for a time to help compensate for inappropriate domestic policies in the past that permitted business confidence to fail and investment in new capacity to be insufficient.

Nevertheless, it would be worthwhile to have, as a medium- to long-term objective, a reduction in reliance upon net capital inflows. Such inflows to Canada could be lowered as capacity increased through new investment and more efficient use of existing physical capital stock via internal rationalization or if the terms of trade should improve for some of the nation's major exports like wheat, forest products, and minerals or as natural gas exports to the United States were greatly expanded and the merchandise trade account strengthened sufficiently to begin reducing the current-account deficit. This would be preferable to letting the Canadian dollar rise again, thereby eroding the improved competitive position that Canada had achieved.

It might be necessary, too, to follow policies similar to Japan's with respect to that country's needs for particular types of machinery and equipment and forecast Canadian needs sufficiently ahead of time so that licenses to produce domestically are obtained. This could be done with respect to the oil sands and heavy-oil development, where the requirements are highly specialized and it is known that development is going to have to proceed.

Note as well that Canada's present foreign exchange reserves are not just $4-5 billion as the official statistics suggest. Included in these reserves are about $1 billion of gold valued at the old — and now irrelevant — price of 35 SDRs an ounce. If these gold reserves were sold at market value, they would be worth about $15 billion. They could be used to cushion any decline in the Canadian dollar that may come from discouraging capital inflows during the period when domestic capacity is being enlarged.

It would not be difficult to lessen net capital inflows as the current-account deficit was reduced, provided there was the will to

---

[18]Statistics Canada, *Daily Bulletin,* May 18, 1979. In the first quarter of 1979 the overall capacity utilization rate for manufacturing of 89.6 percent was approaching the high rates in the first quarter of 1966, the fourth quarter of 1973, and the first quarter of 1974 of 91.7 percent, 91.6 percent, and 93 percent, respectively.

do so. For example, the differential between Canadian and U.S. interest rates could be lowered; this would both reduce capital inflows and encourage Canadian investment. New withholding taxes could be imposed on interest and other payments abroad (rather than removing them, as the federal government has done). Such taxes could be set so that the net after-tax return to foreign lenders would be less than that which such lenders could obtain in their own nations or elsewhere while simultaneously making the interest rate paid by the Canadian borrowing abroad higher than he would pay if borrowing within Canada. Again, interest payments on corporate foreign debt could be disallowed as expenses for income tax purposes, whereas domestic debt charges could be allowed. In other words, even apart from lowering interest rate differentials, a wedge could be driven between U.S. and Canadian costs of capital to discourage foreign borrowing.

Again, direct investment in Canada that represents merely a takeover of an existing firm could be discouraged, if not prevented entirely. Takeovers by Canadian firms of foreign firms operating in Canada, especially in the resource sector, could be encouraged, as could increased direct investment by Canadian firms abroad. The federal government, through the Bank of Canada or some other agency, could redeem provincial, municipal, and even corporate securities from the United States and elsewhere.

Such policies, by keeping down the international value of the Canadian dollar, would also help to break the exchange-rate-parity concept — the view that one Canadian dollar should exchange for one U.S. dollar — and so encourage continued industrial modernization and expansion in Canada. (To be consistent with the other policies suggested, preference in this expansion would be given to Canadian firms or to foreign firms allowing major Canadian participation.)

If, however, the merchandise trade account improved and Canadians persisted in believing that long-term capital inflows were essential, they would see Canada as having no alternative but to let the value of the dollar rise again. The result would be that the strengthening merchandise trade surplus would eventually be diminished and the current-account deficit would expand to equal the capital inflow, thereby seemingly justifying the assumption that the capital inflows were needed. The effectiveness of other policies designed to improve the competitiveness of Canadian industry would also be reduced.

It would not, of course, be possible, or desirable, to choke off all net capital inflows immediately. It takes time to alter procedures, customs, and institutions. Even after changes are made, events such as a poor grain harvest domestically or an exceptionally good harvest in other countries may cause the trade balance to diminish for a season or so. Such situations, however, can be met by short-term borrowing rather than by embarking upon a renewed policy of persistent long-term borrowing. The long-range, underlying policy should be to reduce dependence upon foreign sources of long-term financing.

A policy of moving toward reducing reliance upon capital inflows would also be consistent with the view that wealthy nations like Canada should not be absorbing the world's capital but should be freeing it to find uses in developing countries.

Such a policy would not be detrimental to the U.S. *overall* balance of payments. Although much of Canada's merchandise trade gain would have to come from its trade with the United States, Canada could also argue that, by reducing its dependence upon U.S. long-term capital, there would be no net drain on the U.S. balance of payments. Only the composition of the U.S. balance of payments would be altered, in a manner just opposite to the compositional change for Canada.

Concluding Remarks

The three policies outlined in this chapter — internal rationalization of industry before entering any complete free-trade arrangement, larger tied program grants to developing countries, and diminished dependence upon foreign long-term capital inflows — complement one another. They would help Canada to become economically more efficient, productive, and self-reliant, and the foundations would have been laid for Canada to be better able to participate in, and to benefit from, future trade liberalization. They would also enable Canada to set an example to the wealthy nations of giving greater aid to developing countries without burdening them more heavily with debt.

The road to strengthening the achievements of the Canadian economy will not be easy, regardless of the route taken. Perhaps the greatest danger Canada faces is that politicians and the public will seek solutions that appear to be relatively painless in the short run, thereby only deferring the day when larger and more difficult adjustments will be necessary.

Appendix A

Supplementary Tables

TABLE A.1(a)

Components of Gross National Expenditure, 1952-78
(current 1971 dollars)

	Percentages of Gross National Expenditure					
	1952-56	1957-61	1962-66	1967-71	1972-76	1977-78
	(1)	(2)	(3)	(4)	(5)	(6)
Current outlay:						
Personal consumption	63.4	65.6	62.2	59.5	58.1	58.4
Current government expenditures	14.4	14.1	15.3	18.2	19.7	20.6
	77.7	79.7	77.5	77.7	77.8	79.0
Gross fixed-capital formation:						
Government	3.3	4.1	4.3	4.0	3.7	3.3
Business	14.0	14.2	13.6	13.4	13.7	13.6
Residential housing	5.2	5.2	4.5	4.5	5.5	5.9
	22.5	23.5	22.4	21.9	22.9	22.8
Value of physical change in inventories	1.5	.4	1.7	.7	.9	.3
Total investment	23.9	23.9	24.1	22.6	23.8	23.1
Exports	20.6	18.6	20.2	23.4	25.0	25.9
Imports	-22.4	-21.7	-21.8	-23.6	-26.6	-28.1
Residual error	.2	-.5	—	-.1	—	—
GNE	100.0	100.0	100.0	100.0	100.0	100.0

TABLE A.1(b)

Components of Gross Capital Formation, 1952-78
(current 1971 dollars)

	Percentages of Gross Capital Formation					
	1952-56	1957-61	1962-66	1967-71	1972-76	1977-78
	(1)	(2)	(3)	(4)	(5)	(6)
Gross fixed-capital formation:						
Government	13.7	17.1	17.9	17.7	15.6	14.3
Business	58.0	59.2	56.9	59.2	57.5	59.1
Residential housing	21.8	21.8	18.3	19.9	23.3	25.3
	93.5	98.1	93.1	96.8	96.4	98.7
Value of physical change in inventories	6.5	1.9	7.0	3.3	3.6	1.3
GCF	100.0	100.0	100.0	100.0	100.0	100.0

Source: Department of Finance, *Economic Review*, 1979 (Ottawa, 1979), p. 125.

TABLE A.2(a)

Components of Gross National Expenditure, 1952-78
(constant 1971 dollars)

	Percentages of Gross National Expenditure					
	1952-56	1957-61	1962-66	1967-71	1972-76	1977-78
	(1)	(2)	(3)	(4)	(5)	(6)
Current outlay:						
Personal consumption	59.2	61.8	59.6	58.7	61.1	63.1
Current government expenditures	20.8	18.0	17.9	19.1	19.1	18.0
	80.0	79.8	77.5	77.8	80.2	81.1
Gross fixed-capital formation:						
Government	3.0	4.0	4.3	4.0	3.6	3.2
Business	13.8	13.9	13.4	13.4	14.0	13.9
Residential housing	5.3	5.4	4.6	4.5	5.0	4.8
	22.2	23.3	22.4	22.0	22.6	21.9
Value of physical change in inventories	1.2	.5	1.5	.7	.8	.2
Total investment	23.4	23.7	23.9	22.7	23.4	22.1
Exports	17.5	16.5	18.0	22.5	23.0	23.6
Imports	–20.1	–19.6	–19.6	–23.0	–26.6	–26.9
Residual error	–.8	–.4	.2	—	—	—
GNE	100.0	100.0	100.0	100.0	100.0	100.0

TABLE A.2(b)

Components of Gross Capital Formation, 1952-78
(constant 1971 dollars)

	Percentages of Gross Capital Formation					
	1952-56	1957-61	1962-66	1967-71	1972-76	1977-78
	(1)	(2)	(3)	(4)	(5)	(6)
Gross fixed-capital formation:						
Government	12.7	16.8	18.1	17.8	15.5	14.5
Business	59.2	58.3	56.1	59.2	59.6	62.6
Residential housing	22.9	22.9	19.4	19.9	21.3	21.9
	94.8	98.0	93.6	96.9	96.4	99.0
Value of physical change in inventories	5.2	2.0	6.3	3.1	3.5	1.1
GCF	100.0	100.0	100.0	100.0	100.0	100.0

Source: Department of Finance, *Economic Review*, 1979, p. 127.

TABLE A.3

Composition of Capital Formation, Major Sectors, 1952-78
(current dollars)

	1952-56 (1)	1957-61 (2)	1962-66 (3)	1967-71 (4)	1972-76 (5)	1977-78 (6)
Primary and construction industries:						
Construction	25.1	28.6	30.8	34.2	32.7	35.1
Machinery and equipment	46.0	40.9	42.0	38.0	39.6	39.2
Repairs	28.9	30.5	27.2	27.9	27.7	25.6
	100.0	100.0	100.0	100.0	100.0	100.0
Manufacturing:						
Construction	23.3	20.7	17.6	19.6	18.7	17.6
Machinery and equipment	43.2	44.3	49.6	47.5	48.1	47.5
Repairs	33.4	35.1	32.8	32.8	33.2	34.9
	100.0	100.0	100.0	100.0	100.0	100.0
Utilities:						
Construction	38.6	46.4	43.8	41.3	41.1	41.6
Machinery and equipment	29.0	27.2	28.0	33.8	35.5	34.6
Repairs	32.5	26.4	28.2	24.9	23.5	23.8
	100.0	100.0	100.0	100.0	100.0	100.0
Trade, finance, and commercial services:						
Construction	41.6	45.6	45.1	39.1	44.0	42.4
Machinery and equipment	37.8	37.7	39.5	45.4	45.0	44.9
Repairs	20.6	16.7	15.4	15.5	11.0	12.6
	100.0	100.0	100.0	100.0	100.0	100.0
Institutions:						
Construction	78.7	79.0	78.8	76.7	69.4	64.0
Machinery and equipment	9.8	10.4	13.1	14.6	17.4	18.8
Repairs	11.6	10.6	8.1	8.7	13.2	17.2
	100.0	100.0	100.0	100.0	100.0	100.0
Government departments:						
Construction	69.3	71.1	69.6	70.2	73.7	74.7
Machinery and equipment	7.5	6.8	8.3	8.1	10.2	9.6
Repairs	23.2	22.1	22.1	21.6	16.1	15.8
	100.0	100.0	100.0	100.0	100.0	100.0
Total:						
Construction	40.0	44.4	42.4	42.2	41.6	41.1
Machinery and equipment	31.8	29.6	32.5	33.5	35.5	35.4
Repairs	28.2	26.0	25.1	24.4	22.9	23.6
	100.0	100.0	100.0	100.0	100.0	100.0

Source: Department of Finance, *Economic Review*, 1979, pp. 141-42.

TABLE A.4

Sources of Financing of Gross Capital Formation, 1950-77
(percentages)

	Government			Unincorporated Businesses			Corporate Domestic-Owned Businesses and Government Enterprises			Total of Private Individuals and Domestic Businesses			Non-Residents					Residual Error of Estimate [a] (times 2)	Total Capital Formation	
													Retained Earnings	Net New Inflows	Total	Dep'n	Total		Net [b]	Gross [c]
	Net	Dep'n	Total	Net	Dep'n	Total	Net	Dep'n	Total	Net	Dep'n	Total								
	(1)	(2)	(3)	(4)	(5)	(6)	(7)	(8)	(9)	(10)	(11)	(12)	(13)	(14)	(15)	(16)	(17)	(18)	(19)	(20)
1950	19.3	4.5	23.8	19.7	17.0	36.7	10.0	16.3	26.3	29.7	33.3	63.0	1.4	7.3	8.6	4.7	13.3	.2	57.4	100.0
1951	22.6	4.7	27.3	28.1	15.2	43.4	5.7	15.1	20.8	33.8	30.5	64.3	1.9	9.8	11.7	4.4	16.1	-7.7	60.4	100.0
1952	11.4	4.8	16.2	30.5	15.9	46.4	16.3	16.1	32.3	46.8	31.9	78.7	3.8	-3.2	.5	5.0	5.5	-.4	58.4	100.0
1953	8.8	4.4	13.2	21.9	15.8	37.7	14.2	16.1	30.3	36.1	31.8	67.9	3.9	7.1	11.0	5.3	16.3	2.5	58.5	100.0
1954	5.4	5.3	10.8	14.3	19.7	34.1	17.4	20.9	38.3	31.8	40.7	72.2	4.0	7.6	11.6	7.3	18.9	-1.9	46.9	100.0
1955	8.8	4.8	13.6	12.7	18.7	31.3	15.6	19.3	34.9	28.4	37.9	66.2	4.0	10.3	14.3	7.2	21.4	-1.1	50.4	100.0
1956	11.7	4.1	15.7	12.0	15.1	27.2	12.4	17.3	29.6	24.4	32.4	56.7	3.5	15.3	18.7	6.0	24.8	2.9	57.7	100.0
1957	10.1	4.4	14.5	11.7	15.9	27.6	10.5	20.0	30.4	22.2	35.9	58.1	3.8	16.3	20.1	6.7	26.8	.5	53.1	100.0
1958	-0.7	4.9	4.2	15.4	17.5	32.9	14.8	21.1	35.9	30.2	38.6	68.9	2.3	13.8	16.1	6.7	22.8	4.1	49.8	100.0
1959	6.0	4.7	10.7	9.2	16.6	25.7	12.1	21.5	32.7	20.3	38.1	58.3	3.2	16.3	19.5	6.4	26.0	5.0	50.8	100.0
1960	4.2	5.3	9.5	9.8	18.1	27.9	11.8	23.1	34.9	21.6	41.2	62.8	2.6	13.9	16.3	6.9	23.3	4.4	46.6	100.0
1961	3.8	6.2	10.0	9.0	19.0	28.1	13.2	24.7	37.8	22.2	43.7	65.9	2.5	10.9	13.4	7.4	20.8	3.3	42.7	100.0
1962	6.5	6.0	12.5	17.3	17.4	34.7	12.7	24.2	36.9	29.9	41.6	71.5	2.7	8.7	11.4	7.2	18.6	-2.6	45.2	100.0
1963	7.0	6.2	13.2	17.9	17.3	35.2	12.5	23.9	36.4	30.4	41.2	71.6	3.4	5.1	8.5	7.5	16.0	-.8	45.2	100.0
1964	11.8	5.8	17.6	12.8	16.7	29.4	15.1	22.1	37.2	27.8	38.8	66.7	3.9	3.7	7.6	7.4	14.9	.9	48.0	100.0
1965	13.0	5.3	18.3	13.6	14.8	28.4	12.4	19.3	31.7	26.0	34.1	59.9	4.3	7.8	12.2	6.8	18.9	2.8	54.0	100.0
1966	14.5	5.2	19.7	17.0	14.2	31.2	12.0	18.2	30.2	29.0	32.4	61.0	3.1	7.0	10.1	6.9	17.1	2.2	55.8	100.0
1967	13.9	5.8	19.7	16.6	15.5	32.1	12.8	19.6	32.4	29.4	35.2	64.6	4.2	3.1	7.3	8.0	15.3	.4	51.0	100.0
1968	15.3	6.0	21.3	14.4	15.9	30.3	15.0	19.9	34.8	29.4	35.8	65.2	4.2	.7	4.8	8.5	13.4	.1	49.7	100.0
1969	20.6	5.9	26.6	14.7	14.9	29.6	11.5	18.6	30.1	26.1	33.5	59.7	4.8	4.9	9.7	8.7	18.5	-4.7	51.7	100.0
1970	15.1	6.8	21.9	16.3	15.9	32.3	12.5	20.7	33.2	28.9	36.8	65.5	4.2	-6.1	-1.9	10.7	8.8	3.8	45.9	100.0
1971	11.8	6.3	18.1	16.8	14.6	31.4	10.2	18.4	28.6	27.0	32.9	60.0	5.2	-2.0	3.2	10.3	13.5	8.4	50.4	100.0

1972	10.9	6.4	17.2	21.0	14.2	35.3	10.5	17.8	28.3	31.6	32.0	63.6	5.7	1.6	7.3	10.3	17.6	1.6	51.4	100.0
1973	13.0	5.8	18.8	24.6	13.7	38.3	10.9	16.8	27.7	35.5	30.5	65.9	6.8	-.4	6.5	9.1	15.5	-.3	54.6	100.0
1974	16.2	5.7	21.9	27.0	13.2	40.2	7.5	14.9	22.4	34.4	28.1	62.5	6.8	4.1	10.9	8.4	19.3	-3.8	57.8	100.0
1975	.2	6.2	6.5	30.4	13.5	44.0	7.8	16.2	24.0	38.2	29.7	68.0	5.4	12.0	17.4	9.0	26.4	-.9	55.1	100.0
1976	.7	6.1	6.8	28.9	12.9	41.9	9.7	15.7	25.4	38.6	28.7	67.3	4.5	9.0	13.5	8.7	22.1	3.7	56.5	100.0
1977	3.5	6.0	3.4	30.5	13.9	44.5	4.6	17.4	29.0	42.1	31.3	73.4	5.5	9.2	14.0	9.2	23.2	.1	52.6	100.0

[a] This "residual error" is a balancing item in the *National Accounts* such that all gross savings plus twice the residual error are equal to gross capital formation (see Powrie, p. 72).

[b] Column 19 = columns 1 + 4 + 7 + 15 + 18.

[c] Column 20 = columns 3 + 6 + 9 + 17 + 18.

Source: T. L. Powrie, "The Contribution of Foreign Capital to Canadian Economic Growth," unpublished manuscript, 1977.

TABLE A.5

Profit Rates, Foreign-Owned and Domestic Metal-Mining Firms, 1972-76

(percentages)

	1972		1973		1974		1975		1976	
	Foreign-Owned	Domestic	Foreign-Owned	Domestic	Foreign-Owned	Domestic	Foreign-Owned	Domestic	Foreign-Owned	Domestic
Net profit before tax as percentage of total equity	.01	.12	.17	.28	.13	.34	.06	.18	.06	.15
Net profit after tax as percentage of total equity	.00	.09	.13	.18	.07	.19	.03	.12	.05	.10
Net profit before tax as percentage of capital employed	.00	.08	.11	.19	.09	.24	.04	.13	.04	.09
Average	.003	.096	.137	.217	.097	.257	.043	.143	.05	.113
Foreign firms' return on equity as percentage of domestic firms' return on equity	.03		.63		.377		.30		.44	

Source: Statistics Canada, *Corporations and Labour Unions Returns Act — Part I — Corporations*, 1975 (Ottawa, 1978), Statement 11B, p. 47.

TABLE A.6

Canada's Terms of Trade, 1972-78
(1971 = 100)

Commodity Group	1972	1973	1974	1975	1976	1977	1978
(a) **Net Barter or Commodity Terms of Trade** [a]							
Live animals	113.9	116.0	124.6	97.6	114.1	100.4	92.9
Food, feed, beverages, and tobacco	98.1	113.2	136.2	130.1	133.9	101.2	99.3
Crude materials	95.8	94.3	75.5	69.9	73.0	72.5	73.4
Fabricated materials	105.2	110.2	108.1	112.6	117.4	114.8	110.4
End products	100.0	99.1	99.1	94.0	96.4	93.0	90.1
	101.1	107.1	115.0	110.0	112.2	107.3	103.4
(b) **Gross Barter or Quantity Terms of Trade** [b]							
Live animals	101.3	188.3	265.4	151.0	158.5	59.3	59.9
Food, feed, beverages, and tobacco	107.2	126.7	158.4	154.0	164.6	137.2	132.2
Crude materials	102.2	93.4	94.8	110.2	108.7	107.5	121.0
Fabricated materials	105.7	105.9	120.9	125.3	113.8	101.5	91.9
End products	105.5	110.1	124.0	117.0	110.0	101.2	94.4
	106.8	112.1	128.3	130.9	126.5	116.8	110.6

[a] Price of exports divided by price of imports.
[b] Quantity of imports divided by quantity of exports.

Source: Statistics Canada, *Summary of External Trade* (Ottawa, various issues).

TABLE A.7

Composition and Destinations of Canadian Merchandise Exports, 1964, 1970, and 1978

(percentages)

	United States			Japan			Destination — United Kingdom			EEC[a]			Rest of World			Total		
	1964	1970	1978	1964	1970	1978	1964	1970	1978	1964	1970	1978	1964	1970	1978	1964	1970	1978
Animals, food, feed, beverages, and tobacco	9.2	6.3	4.1	35.2	16.2	25.4	27.8	17.4	22.8	30.0	15.3	16.6	47.0	27.1	27.9	22.7	11.4	10.2
Crude materials (inedible)[b]	14.4	6.9	4.5	33.4	46.9	25.6	21.1	21.3	17.8	27.0	32.8	25.4	7.4	14.6	10.8	15.4	13.1	8.3
Energy products	9.4	9.1	13.8	2.8	4.1	19.6	0.1	0.0	0.4	0.2	0.3	1.7	0.2	0.2	1.5	5.1	6.1	11.2
Fabricated materials[c]	49.1	30.1	30.2	22.0	28.0	24.8	49.8	48.6	41.3	22.8	36.0	37.9	18.0	28.5	21.7	39.3	31.8	29.5
	82.1	52.3	52.6	93.4	95.1	95.4	93.7	87.4	82.3	79.4	84.3	81.6	69.9	70.4	61.9	82.5	62.5	59.2
Road motor vehicles	2.3	30.6	30.9	0.0	0.1	0.1	0.2	0.3	0.5	0.8	0.4	1.1	4.1	9.7	12.9	2.2	21.3	23.7
Other highly manufactured goods[d]	15.6	16.2	16.0	6.6	4.8	4.5	8.1	12.3	16.9	19.8	15.3	17.3	18.7	19.7	25.0	15.2	15.7	16.8
	17.8	46.8	46.9	6.6	4.9	4.6	8.3	12.6	17.4	20.6	15.6	18.4	22.8	29.4	37.9	17.4	37.0	40.5
Special transactions	0.5	0.2	0.4	0.0	0.0	0.0	0.0	0.0	0.2	0.1	0.0	0.1	0.3	0.3	0.2	0.3	0.2	0.3
	100.0	100.0	100.0	100.0	100.0	100.0	100.0	100.0	100.0	100.0	100.0	100.0	100.0	100.0	100.0	100.0	100.0	100.0

[a]Excluding United Kingdom.
[b]Excluding energy products.
[c]Excluding energy products and chemicals.
[d]End products (inedible) plus chemicals, less road motor vehicles.

Source: Statistics Canada, *Summary of External Trade*, various issues.

TABLE A.8

Composition and Sources of Canadian Merchandise Imports, 1964, 1970, and 1978
(percentages)

	United States			Japan			United Kingdom			EEC[a]			Rest of World			Total		
	1964	1970	1978	1964	1970	1978	1964	1970	1978	1964	1970	1978	1964	1970	1978	1964	1970	1978
Animals, food, feed, beverages, and tobacco	7.2	5.2	5.5	5.0	3.1	2.2	6.1	6.7	10.5	8.0	8.2	10.5	29.6	24.4	16.8	10.6	8.0	7.6
Crude materials (inedible)[b]	6.8	3.8	3.4	0.2	0.2	0.3	6.5	3.3	3.2	1.9	1.1	1.9	13.0	9.8	6.4	7.3	4.3	3.6
Energy products	3.1	2.4	4.0	0.1	0.0	0.0	0.6	0.2	0.4	0.3	0.6	0.5	22.6	28.6	39.4	7.5	5.7	9.0
Fabricated materials[c]	15.3	12.7	11.0	42.2	27.2	17.5	25.8	21.4	18.6	28.5	17.3	16.1	5.7	12.4	9.4	15.9	14.0	11.6
	32.4	24.1	23.9	47.5	30.5	20.0	39.0	31.6	31.7	38.7	27.2	29.0	81.9	75.2	72.0	41.3	32.0	31.8
Road motor vehicles	13.5	29.2	34.0	2.4	19.3	30.0	10.2	8.2	4.5	12.5	16.7	11.6	0.5	2.5	1.6	10.9	23.3	26.2
Other highly manufactured goods[d]	50.2	45.4	41.5	48.6	49.4	49.0	49.5	58.7	62.0	47.6	54.5	57.7	17.2	21.6	25.4	44.8	43.6	41.0
	63.7	74.6	75.5	51.0	68.7	79.0	59.7	66.9	66.5	60.1	71.2	69.3	17.7	24.1	27.0	55.7	66.9	67.2
Special transactions	3.8	1.2	0.9	1.6	0.8	1.0	1.3	1.5	1.6	1.2	1.6	1.6	0.5	0.7	0.8	2.9	1.2	1.0
	100.0	100.0	100.0	100.0	100.0	100.0	100.0	100.0	100.0	100.0	100.0	100.0	100.0	100.0	100.0	100.0	100.0	100.0

[a]Excluding United Kingdom.
[b]Excluding energy products.
[c]Excluding energy products and chemicals.
[d]End products (inedible) plus chemicals, less road motor vehicles.
Source: Statistics Canada, *Summary of External Trade*, various issues.

TABLE A.9

**Shares of Canadian Exports and Highly Manufactured Exports in
Selected Countries' Imports, 1967 and 1977**
(percentages)

	Destination							
	United States		Japan		United Kingdom		EEC[a]	
	1967	1977	1967	1977	1967	1977	1967	1977
Share of Canadian exports in imports of country of destination	26.5	20.1	5.4	4.1	7.1	3.4	1.2	.9
Share of Canadian highly manufactured exports[b] in imports of country of destination	28.1	23.8	2.5	1.2	2.9	1.2	.3	.2

[a] Excluding the United Kingdom.
[b] SITC groups 5, 7, and 8.

Source: Organisation for Economic Co-operation and Development, *Market Summaries: Imports*, 1967 and 1977 (Paris, 1969 and 1979), Series C.

Appendix B

A Comparison of Several Total-Factor-Productivity Estimates for Canada

Total factor productivity refers to the growth in output per unit of labor and capital inputs, where these inputs are appropriately weighted so that they can be aggregated. Adjustments may be introduced in the computations for the impact of reduced hours of work, age, sex, level of education and training, and the legal and institutional environment upon the quantity and/or quality of labor input. Adjustments for quality improvements in the capital stock and estimates of the relative importance of influences — such as economies of scale and improved allocation of resources — affecting the growth in output per unit of total factor input are sometimes made as well.

Studies for Canada vary somewhat in their methods of estimating the changes in basic factor inputs as well as in the extent to which other elements are taken into account. Some difficulties in comparison also arise because time spans differ and because the official statistics upon which the work is based are revised periodically.[1]

Tables B.1 and B.2 summarize the results of several researchers. Perhaps the most important point demonstrated by the numbers is that we should not be too adamant about the precise contribution made to growth by labor, capital, and residual elements. Results are very much a function of the assumptions employed. For example, although in the study by Christensen and Cummings (see Table B.1, column 7), which spans roughly the two periods measured by Walters (see Table B.1, columns 5 and 6), the *total* growth rate of output is

---

[1] For detailed discussion of the problems arising in productivity investigations and comparisons over time and among countries, see M. I. Nadiri, "Some Approaches to the Theory of Measurement of Total Factor Productivity: A Survey," *Journal of Economic Literature* 8 (1967): 1137-77, and I. B. Kravis, "A Survey of International Comparisons of Productivity," *Economic Journal* 86 (March, 1976): 1-44. Attempts to estimate the sensitivity of outcomes to diverse valuations of labor, capital, and output are made in J. D. May and M. Denny, "On the Sensitivity of Productivity Measures in Canadian Manufacturing," paper presented at the Canadian Economics Association meetings, June, 1977; see also their "Testing Productivity Models," Working Paper Series No. 7805, Institute for Policy Analysis, University of Toronto, February, 1978.

TABLE B.1

Comparison of Sources of Canadian Economic Growth, Various Periods
(percentage-point contribution to growth rates)

	Lithwick				Walters		Christensen and Cummings, 1947-73
	1891-1910	1910-26	1926-56	1956-66	1950-62	1962-67	
	(1)	(2)	(3)	(4)	(5)	(6)	(7)
National output	3.38	2.46	3.89	4.18	4.8	6.0	5.1
Factor inputs:							
Labor	1.82	.98	.62	1.17	1.5	2.7	.9
Employment			1.22	1.98	1.5	2.6	.6
Hours worked			-.63	-.60	-.2	-.2	
Age-sex composition			-.09	-.30	-.1	-.2	
Education			.2	.09	.3	.5	.3
Capital	.81	.31	.46	.67	1.2	1.1	2.5
Housing			.03	.05	.3	.3	
Other construction			.20	.52			
Machinery and equipment			.20	.13	.9	.8	
Inventories			.06	.07	.1	.1	
Net domestic capital			.49	.77	1.3	1.2	1.9
Canadian capital abroad			.02	.02			
Foreign capital in Canada			-.05	-.12	-.1	-.2	
Quality of capital							.6
	2.63	1.30	1.09	1.84	2.7	3.8	3.4
Total factor productivity	.75	1.16	2.80	2.34	2.1	2.3	1.8
Improved allocation of resources			.66[a]		.7	.5	
Decline in agricultural imports					.6	.4	
Decline in non-agricultural self-employment					.1	.1	

Economies of scale	.6	.7
Growth in national market	.5	.6
Growth in local market	.1	.1
Income elasticities in consumption	—	.1
Other adjustments	.2	.2
Residual sources of growth	.6	.8
	2.80	2.34

[a] For 1937-61, primarily because of the shift out of agriculture into manufacturing and other higher-productivity sectors; but this is not subtracted from total factor productivity to arrive at the residual sources of growth. Lithwick estimated that this shift accounted for 21 percent of aggregate growth over these years.

Sources: Columns 1-4: N. H. Lithwick, *Economic Growth in Canada: A Quantitative Analysis*, 2nd ed. (Toronto: University of Toronto Press, 1970), pp. 53 and 60.
Columns 5-6: Dorothy Walters, *Canadian Growth Revisited, 1950-1967* (Ottawa: Economic Council of Canada, 1970), p. 37.
Column 7: Laurits R. Christensen and Diane Cummings, "Real Product, Real Factor Input, and Productivity in Canada, 1947-1973," mimeographed (Madison: Social Systems Research Institute, University of Wisconsin, 1976).

TABLE B.2

Relative Contributions of Labor, Capital, and Total Factor Productivity to Growth in Canadian Output, Various Periods
(percentages)

	Lithwick				Walters and Economic Council			Christensen and Cummings, 1947-73
	1891-1910	1910-26	1926-56	1956-66	1950-62	1962-67	1966-73	
	(1)	(2)	(3)	(4)	(5)	(6)	(7)	(8)
National output	100.0	100.0	100.0	100.0	100.0	100.0	100.0	100.0
Factor inputs:								
Labor	53.8	39.8	15.9	28.0	31.3	45.0	50.0	17.6
Capital	23.9	12.6	12.0	16.0	25.0	18.3	20.0	49.0
	77.8	52.8	28.0	44.0	56.3	63.3	70.0	66.7
Total factor productivity	22.2	47.2	72.0	56.0	43.7	36.7	30.0	33.3

Sources: Columns 1-6 and 8: Appendix Table B.1.
Column 7: Economic Council of Canada, *Twelfth Annual Review* (Ottawa, 1975), Table 3-1.

about the average of the results for the two periods studied by Walters, the relative importance of factor inputs is somewhat greater. Even more noteworthy is the much reduced relative importance of labor inputs in the Christensen-Cummings work and the much larger role of capital. This result is apparently a function of counting *all* expenditures on consumer durables (not just housing) as investment rather than as consumption and of allowing for quality improvements in capital. Accordingly, the role of capital, and hence of total factor inputs, in economic growth is expanded. Neither the Lithwick nor the Walters study uses the same methods.

The Lithwick numbers are particularly useful because they provide a longer-run view of the growth process, extending back to before the turn of the century, and are based on a consistent methodology for each period. The declining role of both labor and capital inputs up to the 1950s and the increase thereafter are evident, as are the negative effects of reduced hours of work and the changing age-sex composition of the labor force. Also of note is the significance for output growth of sectoral shifts in economic activity (the movement of resources out of agriculture into more productive industries being the primary one). These shifts were apparently responsible for from one-eighth to one-fifth of output expansion to about 1960.

Of particular interest in Walters' estimates (see Table B.2), which were updated by the Economic Council of Canada for 1966-73 (as was also evident from the estimates in Table 7), is the increase in the relative importance of labor inputs and the reduction in total factor productivity between 1952 and 1973.

Appendix C

Summary Results of a Constant-Market-Share Analysis of Canadian Export Growth, 1970-74 [1]

Changes over time in a nation's market share of world exports can be categorized as occurring for three basic reasons:[2]

- because the commodity composition of exports differs from the average composition of world exports;

- because the mix of country destinations of exports differs from the average mix of destinations of world exports;

- because a nation's competitive position diverges from that of its trading partners.

Estimates of the relative significance of these factors for Canada for the years 1970-74 are as follows:

	Amount (bil. U.S. $)
• Total increase in Canadian exports between 1970 and 1974	= 16.6
• Increase in Canadian exports that would have occurred if Canada had retained a constant share of world markets	= 27.6
• Difference to be "explained"	= 11.0

"Explanation":

a) Commodity composition effect: loss in sales because of Canadian emphasis upon products for which markets were growing more slowly than the average for all products ... = −2.3

---

[1] This appendix relies upon James E. Powell, "A Constant Market Share Analysis of Canadian Export Growth: 1970-1974," Department of Economics, University of Alberta, March, 1978.

[2] For a discussion of the methodology used in this analysis, see E. Leamer and R. Stern, *Quantitative International Economics* (Boston: Allyn and Bacon, 1970), Chap. 7.

b) Market distribution effect: gain in sales owing to
    Canadian emphasis upon exports to countries
    whose imports were growing faster than the
    world average   =   .3

c) Competitive effect: loss in sales resulting from all
    other factors influencing exports   = −9.0
                                                               ─────
                                                               −11.0
                                                               ═════

   Results are somewhat different, however, if the market effect is
estimated before the commodity effect:

a) Commodity composition effect   = −1.1

b) Market distribution effect   =   −.9

c) Competitive effect   = −9.0
                                                               ─────
                                                               −11.0
                                                               ═════

   Note that the latter approach causes the market distribution effect to change from a small positive figure to a substantial negative
one and reduces the size of the negative commodity composition effect. It does not, however, alter the large negative competitive effect.

   In his analysis of these results, Powell argues that the competitive effect may be attributable in large measure to inadequate investment during this period and the preceding three years. As we
suggested in the text (particularly in Chapters 4 and 5), a host of
factors are behind this lack of investment, including all the influences affecting Canada's comparative advantage.

Appendix D

Reservations about a Canadian-U.S. Free-Trade Arrangement at This Time

Introduction[1]

The Tokyo Round of GATT negotiations, just concluded as this monograph was completed, promises a range of tariff reductions among the developed nations of the world and possibly some restrictions on non-tariff barriers. It is difficult to assess at this time how important the lowering of trade barriers will be for Canada. In any event, this development is unlikely to cause a cessation of studies and discussion in Canada of the possibility of negotiating some sort of free-trade arrangement with the United States, with which 70 percent of Canada's trade is conducted.[2] In the final volume of the Canada-U.S. Prospects series, of which this study is a part, a more comprehensive survey of future alternatives for Canada and the United States will be undertaken. Here the focus is on one option — Canadian-U.S. free trade — and upon a number of reservations that, in the author's view, have been given insufficient attention.

---

[1] This appendix draws in part upon several other papers by the author: "L'impact d'une zone de libre-échange entre le Canada et les États-Unis : examen critique de l'étude de Wonnacott," *L'Actualité économique*, October-December, 1976, pp. 473-88; "Canada's Trade Options," *The Ryerson Lectures in Economics* (Toronto: Ryerson Polytechnical Institute, 1978); "Canada's Mineral Trade: Implications for the Balance of Payments and Economic Development," in Queen's University, Centre for Resource Studies, *Canada's Mineral Trade, the Balance of Payments and Economic Development*, Proceedings No. 4 (Kingston, Ontario, 1978); and "Notes for the Conference — A North American Common Market: A Realistic Option for Canada," paper presented to the Conference sponsored by the Faculty of Management Studies, University of Toronto, Toronto, November 30-December 1, 1978.

[2] The most recent study is that of the Standing Senate Committee on Foreign Affairs, *Canada-United States Relations*, Vol. 2, *Canada's Trade Relations with the United States* (Ottawa: Queen's Printer, 1978). Recent U.S. discussion of the possibility comes from the U.S. Senate Finance Committee, as reported in H. Solomon, "Free Trade: U.S. Senators Pitch for Trade Bloc with Canada, Mexico," *Financial Post*, May 12, 1978.

Other Canadian studies of recent vintage are: R. J. Wonnacott, *Canada's Trade Options* (Ottawa: Economic Council of Canada, 1975); Economic Council of Canada, *Looking Outward* (Ottawa, 1975); Jim Williams, *The Canadian-United States Tariff and Canadian Industry* (Toronto: University of Toronto Press, 1978); and D. Daly and S. Globerman, *Tariff and Science Policies: Applications of a Model of Nationalism* (Toronto: Ontario Economic Council, 1976).

Expected Benefits

The Economies-of-Scale Argument

A standard argument is that Canada is one of the very few industrial nations lacking free access to a market of at least 100 million people and is therefore limited in the extent to which it can achieve either economies of scale or specialization in production. Hence bilateral free trade is proposed as a means of facilitating the rationalization of manufacturing industry within Canada and across the Canadian-U.S. border, thus permitting greater specialization and longer production runs. Greater productivity, reduced unit costs of production, cheaper prices for consumers, and smaller capital costs per unit of output and per unit of labor, with an accompanying decline in the need for foreign capital inflows, are expected to result — at least once the initial restructuring of industry is complete.

A number of observations need to be made about this argument. First, contemporary research suggests that, excluding automobiles and petroleum products, about 70 percent of consumer products (measured by value) could be manufactured locally in optimal-sized plants if the population were about one million and about 20 percent could still be efficiently produced locally for centers of only 200,000 people.[3] Second, it has been found that, using the conventional technology of major firms, the unit costs of production for a wide range of industries would generally rise much less than 10 percent if plants *one-third* the accepted minimal optimal scale were constructed.[4] Since transportation costs from foreign places of production frequently average well above 10 percent, local factories of smaller size could be quite competitive. Third, other research suggests that cost reductions can be achieved at much smaller scale than is frequently observed. All too often, scale has been dictated by the technology of the large transnational corporation and may not be as rigid as once thought.[5]

These observations give one reason for being skeptical about whether the achievement of economies of scale is as important an argument for free trade as it is sometimes made out to be. Much rationalization could obviously take place in Canada whether or not tariffs are reduced. In those instances where a region is large enough, it could occur on a regional basis. In other instances it could be on a national basis. Free trade, then, may not be essential for much rationalization to occur. It is simply a means of forcing upon domestic industry changes that Canadians themselves are reluctant to bring about.

[3] Barry A. Stein, "Decentralizing the American Economy," in Harold S. Williams, ed., *The Uses of Smallness* (Emmaus, Penn.: Rodale Press, 1978).
[4] F. M. Scherer, "The Determinants of Industrial Plant Sizes in Six Nations," *Review of Economics and Statistics* 55 (May, 1973): 137-38.
[5] Rein Peterson, *Small Business: Building a Balanced Economy* (Erin, Ontario: Press Porcepic, 1977), Chap. 3.

A second reservation regarding the economies-of-scale argument is that total productivity gains may not be nearly as great as they are often expected to be. Consider the farm machinery industry, in which Canada has maintained tariff-free imports since 1944, even to the extent of allowing tariff-free inflows of office equipment for domestic implement manufacturers. It is true that complete bilateral free trade does not exist in this sector because the United States restricts tariff-free imports of tractors, auxiliary equipment, and many parts to those clearly used only for agricultural purposes, and it is not easy to prove to U.S. customs officers that imports are for these purposes.[6] But free entry of such items *into Canada* is allowed. Consequently, according to the standard free-trade argument, one would have expected the lack of Canadian protection to spur a rise in productivity levels to U.S. standards and to cause all domestic firms with lower productivity to be eliminated.

Yet what are the facts? One careful study of the 15-20 percent productivity gap between Canada and the United States in this industry showed that the gap did not close between 1947 and 1966 and in fact, by some measures of labor productivity, actually widened over these years.[7] An update of this study for 1973-74 showed Canadian output per labor unit as still only 78-87 percent of U.S. levels, depending upon the measure of productivity used.[8]

Again, unrestricted imports have not wiped out all small plants that by most engineering standards would be considered to be operating at below optimal scale.[9] In fact, between 1966 and 1975 the very small farm machinery firms of less than 50 employees increased in number by 36 percent, and their share of total employment in the agricultural implement industry rose from 6.5 percent to 8.8 percent.[10] Apparently these firms are able to operate successfully in local, regional, and neighboring U.S. markets — for they do export to the United States[11] — by incurring minimal transport costs compared with larger, more distant producers, by providing a product differentiated by personal contact and service, and/or by meeting the specialized needs of purchasers.

---

[6] Prairie Implement Manufacturers Association, "A Brief to the Standing Senate Committee on Foreign Affairs in Canadian Relations with the United States," *Proceedings of the Standing Senate Committee on Foreign Affairs*, June 7, 1977 (Ottawa: Queen's Printer, 1977), Appendix 23A. See also Standing Senate Committee on Foreign Affairs, *op. cit.*, pp. 66-68.

[7] Christopher J. Maule, *Productivity in the Farm Machinery Industry*, Study No. 3 prepared for the Royal Commission on Farm Machinery (Ottawa: Queen's Printer, 1969), Table 7.

[8] A. N. Book and P. Kampouris, *Statistics Relating to Farm Machinery in Canada, 1950-1976* (Ottawa: Agriculture Canada, 1977), Tables 29A and 29B.

[9] But not as far below as one might expect. In 1975, firms with fewer than 50 employees had value added per employee equal to 86 percent of the level in those firms with over 1,000 employees! (Book and Kampouris, *op. cit.*, Table 27A.)

[10] *Ibid.*, Table 20.

[11] Prairie Implement Manufacturers Association, *op. cit.*

It would appear that the elimination of tariffs has not produced the restructuring of the industry and the productivity increase that it was supposed to. Some may argue that unlimited access to the U.S. market would finally cause Canadian productivity to rise to U.S. levels. But this argument still does not really explain why the average productivity gap remains so large in the farm machinery industry, since, even in the mid-1960s, 75-80 percent of shipments were handled by the four large firms in the industry, who should have been able to rationalize across the border quite effectively, even with the existing U.S. tariff provisions.

Note too that the elimination of Canadian tariffs did not prevent the large multinational firms from setting prices of tractors in Canada well above prices in the United Kingdom plus transportation costs to Canada.[12]

Free trade will not resolve the problem of provincial protectionism either. Where the efficient scale of production is larger than local or individual provincial markets, policies requiring manufacturers to build a plant within provincial boundaries before being able to obtain government contracts, or giving preference on bids to provincial firms over firms located in other parts of Canada, will reduce the productivity gains otherwise achievable through bilateral trade liberalization.

These remarks suggest that some caution needs to be exercised in formulating estimates of the productivity gains likely to emanate from free-trade inducements to greater scale and specialization. They also suggest that, of the possible gains, many may well be achievable through domestic rationalization measures and other policies quite apart from, or perhaps as a preparatory step in anticipation of, free trade.

Greater Technological Advance

A second argument for the elimination of trade restrictions with the United States is that an open U.S. market and the tariff-free inflow of products will provide the incentive and stimulus for more rapid technological diffusion within Canadian industry and for more domestic R & D, thereby helping to rectify Canada's unspectacular R & D performance and to improve the productivity and real incomes of Canadians.

Here again this argument may overstate the case. On the one hand, there are instances — the best example being the Canadian iron and steel industry — where a lack of free trade has not prevented an industry from having a rapid diffusion of new technology

---

[12] Neil B. MacDonald *et al.*, *Farm Tractor Production Costs*, Study No. 2 prepared for the Royal Commission on Farm Machinery (Ottawa: Queen's Printer, 1969).

and becoming competitive by world standards.[13] (Nor was massive foreign ownership instrumental in the success of the iron and steel industry, since this industry is unique among the manufacturing sector in Canada for its high — almost total — Canadian ownership.) On the other hand, some large firms have argued that, if left to themselves, they will continue to carry out their R & D in the United States, where they are frequently closer to their major buyers and where they already have their R & D facilities.[14] Free trade is unlikely to change this aspect of their operations, even if they do undertake rationalization of their productive facilities across the border. In the auto sector the large producers now carry out all their R & D in the United States; this sector undertakes less R & D now than before the auto pact came into being.

In brief, free trade will not, by itself, necessarily produce the level of R & D and the rate of technological advance in Canadian industry that exist in the United States; nor is free trade the only circumstance under which technological change can occur in Canada.

Capitalizing on Comparative Advantage

Various studies have identified Canada's non-replenishable resource endowments as the major source of its comparative advantage in both primary and secondary manufacturing.[15] A third argument for free trade is thus that elimination of escalated foreign tariffs on manufactured resource products will mean additional processing of Canadian mineral resources prior to their exportation. Yet it does not follow that with free trade the amount of Canadian processing for either internal or foreign consumption will immediately rise. A few illustrations should suffice to clarify this view.

First, if tariffs were all-important, one would expect to have seen some expansion in the proportion of Canadian minerals exported in processed form over the past two or three decades as domestic and foreign nominal and effective tariffs were lowered through earlier GATT negotiations.[16] The lower Canadian tariffs should have provided the inducement for domestic processors to look beyond the home market, while the diminished foreign tariffs should have lessened the obstacles to the export of fabricated goods. Yet

---

[13]H. Baumann, "The Relative Competitiveness of the Canadian and U.S. Steel Industries, 1955-1970," *Economic Internazionale*, February, 1974, pp. 141-56.

[14]Standing Senate Committee on Foreign Affairs, *op. cit.*, pp. 53-58.

[15]Harry H. Postner, *Factor Content of Canadian International Trade: An Input-Output Analysis* (Ottawa: Economic Council of Canada, 1975).

[16]For example, Canadian effective tariffs on all groups of processed minerals declined significantly between 1961 and 1970, except for copper and alloys rolling, casting and extruding, and ornamental and architectural metals (B. Wilkinson and K. Norrie, *Effective Protection and the Return to Capital* [Ottawa: Queen's Printer, 1975], Table A-1).

this has not generally occurred, for — as was noted in Chapter 5 — the proportion of Canadian minerals exported in crude form has changed little over the past two decades and is even higher than in the late 1920s. Where a substantial rise in processed exports has transpired, as with iron and steel products, it does not appear that foreign tariffs were consistently lower than for processed products of other minerals.[17] Forces other than tariffs were obviously at work.

Second, the fact that the multinationals, with their processing facilities already in the United States, often prefer to locate near markets for specialized products; the possibility of a free-trade arrangement breaking down; higher capital costs in Canada; the growing protectionism of U.S. labor unions; the pull of manufacturing to the southern states from the northeast (which is adjacent to the main Canadian center of manufacturing) — all suggest that free trade *alone* may not be sufficient to bring about greater mineral processing in Canada. Also, the willingness of developing countries with new, high-quality resources to accept lower pollution standards and low prices if necessary in order to obtain foreign exchange for their own continued development will make these countries important competitors in the U.S. market, even with free Canadian access to that market.

The Fresh Winds of Competition

During 1971-72, debate was at its peak in the United Kingdom as to whether that country should enter the EEC. The major argument that proponents of joining fell back upon (for economies of scale, R & D, and greater mineral processing were relatively unimportant arguments there) was that joining would "expose industry to the fresh winds of competition." Yet today, more than six years after Britain united with the EEC, there is still much inefficiency in manufacturing, and the nation continues to have great difficulty facing international competition. The balance of trade has been strengthened primarily because of the fortunate shift to domestic oil and gas resources, not because of any rapid improvement in the performance of manufacturing *per se*.

One may wish to discount the significance of this particular experience with free trade by pointing to the uncooperative performance of labor, inappropriate monetary and fiscal policies, lack of management initiatives, and so on, but this simply emphasizes the point being made: free-trade arrangements, by themselves, do not necessarily result in the restructuring of industry or in other efficiency-improving measures. Nor do they necessarily eliminate the need for such measures. They are not a panacea for faltering industry. For free trade to be successful, Canada, like Britain, would have

---

[17] Wilkinson, "Canada's Mineral Trade," *op. cit.*, Table 4.

to make many internal adjustments and changes involving the reduction of provincial protectionism, improved attitudes to work, development of management expertise and initiative, and so on. A number of these changes could also be carried out without free trade and thus better prepare the nation to take full advantage of future trade liberalization arrangements.

The focus thus far has been upon the benefits to Canada from free trade. But what are the costs? In the remainder of this section some of the potentially major costs will be considered.

Potential Costs

Control of Resources

An obvious first question is, What autonomy and negotiating power would Canada have to surrender with respect to its non-replaceable natural resource and water endowments in order to gain U.S. acquiescence to complete trade liberalization? The United States cannot gain much in the way of greater efficiency, since it already possesses a large internal market where economic rationalization of manufacturing has taken place and, as opportunities arise, will presumably continue to occur, whether or not a Canadian-U.S. free-trade agreement is entered into.

Although in a number of instances they may now be of lower quality than those becoming available in other lands, Canada's endowments of natural resources (including water) hold out the advantage for the United States of being from a closer and more secure source of supply.

Would Canada have to make commitments of a long-run nature with respect to quantities and prices? What leeway would Canada have to raise prices — as it has on natural gas exports — as world supply conditions changed or to extract the economic rents on these resources for the benefit of Canadians? Would Canada have to surrender all freedom to enter international cartels and to engage in state-trading (as has to be done now with many Latin American and Communist states) and, if so, what would be the costs of doing so? These questions need answers before an unqualified endorsement of free trade can be given.

Canada's Standing Senate Committee on Foreign Affairs, in proposing a free-trade arrangement between Canada and the United States, stated that each nation should be permitted to regulate the speed of exploitation of its own resources and thus restrict exports of them if this is deemed desirable. But it never really broached, let alone answered, the question of what might induce the United States to endorse complete Canadian-U.S. trade liberalization if natural resources were excluded.[18]

---

[18] Standing Senate Committee on Foreign Affairs, *op. cit.*, p. 123.

Foreign Ownership and/or Control

Fairly widespread agreement exists between those who favor moving quickly into free trade and those who suggest a more cautious approach that, *in the short run*, the outcome of such an arrangement probably would be greater foreign influence and/or ownership and control over the Canadian economy. The proportion of Canadian trade with the United States would probably expand from the present level of 70 percent, so that, from this perspective alone, greater dependence upon U.S. policy- and decision-making would ensue. The removal of tariff and non-tariff barriers to trade would also mean that taxes would become a more important determinant of trade.[19] Hence Canada would have even less leeway than it now has in legislating corporate income taxes different from those in the United States.

Again, the high degree of foreign, especially U.S., ownership of Canadian industry in both resource extraction and manufacturing and the fact that foreign corporations are generally larger, more powerful financially, have greater borrowing privileges, possess stronger R & D organizations, and have well-established marketing channels imply that, in the absence of domestic policies to the contrary, foreign firms are likely to be the ones surviving the rationalization and consolidation moves, especially in manufacturing. One may see on the international level what has sometimes been witnessed on a domestic, regional level; for example, in the flour-milling industry, small plants and firms were bought out and closed down, and their former markets were served by the larger parent operation. Accordingly, more of the final decisions affecting the Canadian economy with regard to the location of production, commodities manufactured, exports, imports, R & D, and employment expansion and contraction would be made in head offices situated in the United States.

In the long run, one position is that foreign influence and ownership should decline as production becomes more efficient, capital/output ratios diminish, and income and savings increase. This view, however, ignores the fact that the higher level of trade and fiscal integration would remain. And it ignores that there is no clear reason why, or mechanism whereby, the accumulated foreign control would be diminished. For one thing, a sizable amount of any increased savings will belong to the foreign firms. For another — and this is more important — expanded consumer savings may well result, at best, in greater minority shareholder interest in multinational firms and not necessarily in any change in where the final authority lies. So it may not follow that, in the long run, free trade in itself will result

---

[19] J. R. Melvin, *The Tax Structure and Canadian Trade* (Ottawa: Economic Council of Canada, 1975).

in greater independence and domestic control of Canadian industry and resources. In fact, the opposite could occur.

Reference to the two situations where a form of free trade exists — agricultural machinery and automobiles and parts — may be useful, although the data are limited. The agricultural implement category in the official statistics includes other heavy-equipment manufacture, so the proportion of foreign ownership and control in this industry tends to be overstated.[20] The numbers that are available, however, show that for 1954-75, inclusive, foreign ownership in this sector increased from 37 percent to 59 percent (it reached 68 percent in 1973), while foreign control expanded from 35 percent to 61 percent (it reached 64 percent in 1964).[21] CALURA data[22] indicate that in 1965-67 only about 25 percent of the assets and equity in this sector belonged to the agricultural machinery industry itself. Therefore, it is possible for foreign penetration in the agricultural segment to decline even as the total percentages rise. However, for the years 1965-67, when the agricultural sector was reported separately by CALURA, the percentage of equity owned by foreigners remained close to 53 percent. So the matter is left rather vague. All one can say is that there is no clear evidence that the proportion of foreign ownership in the industry has declined in the long run, and in fact it may have increased. Concurrently, there has certainly been a greater concentration of decision-making in the United States.

In the automotive sector, vehicle manufacturers are not segregated from parts manufacturers. As in the case of farm machinery, decision-making by the large producers has been increasingly concentrated in the United States. Less is known about parts producers. Since 1965-66, foreign ownership of the entire industry has remained at about 88 percent, although it fell a few percentage points below this level in 1971-72; and foreign control has held at 96 percent, although it reached 98 percent in 1969.[23] In the decade since the auto pact, therefore, there does not seem to have been any general tendency for foreign ownership and control to diminish. (Their already preponderant position in the automotive sector has meant that there has not been much scope for increase.)

Thus, the issue of what will happen to foreign ownership and control under free trade has to remain unsettled, but enough has been said to suggest that a healthy wariness about claims that they will necessarily diminish is appropriate.

---

[20]Statistics Canada, *Canada's International Investment Position, 1968-1970* (Ottawa, 1975), Table 31.

[21]*Ibid.* and Statistics Canada, *Daily Bulletin*, December 21, 1978.

[22]Statistics Canada, *Corporations and Labour Unions Returns Act — Part I — Corporations, 1967* (Ottawa, 1969).

[23]Statistics Canada, *Daily Bulletin*, December 21, 1978.

Industrial Location and Trade Flows

In the preceding sections a variety of reasons have been mentioned as to why processing firms may find it attractive to locate in the United States rather than in Canada in the event of trade barriers being removed. These included such factors as the possibility of a free-trade arrangement collapsing; the desire to be close to, and within the national boundaries of, the larger market; and the growing attractiveness for industrial activity of the U.S. South.

It is easy to dismiss these types of arguments by pointing out that with a flexible exchange rate, if production and the trade balance seemed to be swaying in favor of the United States, the Canadian dollar would decline until a new equilibrium was reached and Canada once again became a desirable industrial location. However, because the foreign exchange value of the Canadian dollar has varied considerably vis-à-vis the U.S. dollar over the past two or three decades, primarily because of inappropriate monetary policies formulated with little apparent regard for their effects upon merchandise trade flows, industrialists might hesitate to base longer-term decisions about the best location to serve the North American market, or a portion thereof, upon narrow cost advantages provided by a Canadian dollar below parity with the U.S. dollar unless it was clearly demonstrated that an improved merchandise trade performance was indeed a Canadian priority and that the Canadian dollar would be held down long enough for the decisions to be justified.

Once again, the records for the farm machinery and automotive industries are of interest even though, to repeat, free trade is not complete in these industries. For farm machinery the Canadian trade deficit increased from a little less than $100 million annually, on average, in 1950-54 to about $200 million in 1970-74. The Canadian share of total Canadian and U.S. production diminished from 7.7 percent in 1950-54 to 6.7 percent in 1970-74. (It was even lower in the interim period — 4.7 percent in 1960-64, for example.)[24] For the automotive sector the results are similar, with Canada's share of North American production decreasing in recent years, and a substantial, cumulative deficit occurring since 1965.

Whether complete free trade in these industries, as well as in all other industries, might produce different results is difficult to say. In any event, one should not expect free trade alone to produce great gains in the merchandise trade balance or in the location of industrial activity in Canada.

Economic to Political Integration?

What has been written so far suggests that the gains to Canada from free trade with the United States are probably not as great as

---

[24]Book and Kampouris, *op. cit.*, pp. 101-04.

they have sometimes been made out to be[25] and that there may be a number of serious costs. Hence Canadians should hold more modest expectations with respect to the fruits of Canadian-U.S. trade liberalization. Otherwise they may sell themselves short in any negotiations that may transpire.

Those who are enthusiastic about free trade at this time are generally aware that, in itself, it will not resolve all the problems of Canadian manufacturing and that in some cases the benefits may be of a rather mixed nature. However, their position tends to be that free-trade negotiations should nevertheless go forward and that adjustment assistance policies of various types will usually produce the other changes in Canadian industry that may be necessary.[26]

One final reservation needs to be sounded. It goes beyond anything said so far, and certainly far beyond anything that advocates of complete Canadian-U.S. trade liberalization are willing to accept as a realistic possibility. Still, I believe it should be said.

A Canadian-U.S. free-trade arrangement could be a big step toward eventual political integration. This is not an original thought, and Americans are not oblivious to this possibility. Recall that often-cited, and generally resented, statement by a former U.S. Undersecretary of State, George Ball:

> Canada, I have long believed, is fighting a rearguard action against the inevitable.... Sooner or later, commercial imperatives will bring about free movement of all goods back and forth across our long border; and when that occurs, or even before it does, it will become unmistakably clear that countries with economies so inextricably intertwined must also have free movement of the other vital factors of production — capital, services and labor. The result will inevitably be substantial economic integration, which will require for its full realization a progressively expanding area of common political decision.[27]

It is certainly true that if, via successful U.S.-owned transnational corporations, a greater proportion of final decision-making affecting all aspects of the Canadian economy is made in the United States, it will be only natural for some to argue that an effective way to have a greater voice in these decisions would be through political affiliation and eventual union. A common currency area or full political union might be seen by others as a key step toward resolving the balance of payments problem associated with servicing and repaying Canada's international debt, about 80 percent of which is held in the United States,[28] or toward reducing the massive foreign exchange costs of the travel deficit, which may amount to $5-6

---

[25]Such as 5-10 percent of GNP, as in the Wonnacott estimate (Wonnacott, *op. cit.,* especially Chap. 15).

[26]See Daly and Globerman, *op. cit.,* especially pp. 61-67.

[27]George Ball, *Discipline of Power* (Boston: Little, Brown, 1968), p. 113.

[28]A common currency area would not, of course, ameliorate any difficulties surrounding the extraction of funds from the populace to make the payments.

billion with the United States alone in the mid-1980s. Still others may feel that the two economies and cultures are already so closely integrated that more formal ties are a logical next step.[29]

Continued travel to the United States and the expanding amount of Canadian direct investment there will increase Canadians' familiarity with the people of that nation and may reduce apprehension about a more intimate association of the two countries. If free trade does not permit unlimited migration to the United States from Canada, then, as industry is attracted south, political union may be envisaged by Canadians as a means of gaining this freedom to emigrate. The separation of Quebec from Canada would certainly cause Western Canada and the Maritimes to think seriously about joining the United States.

In the United States, political union of some sort might be seen as a superior means of acquiring assured access to Canada's minerals, water, oil sands, and Arctic. The big deficits the United States must face on energy, combined with the possibility of shifting to imports from Canada rather than from OPEC by means of massive investments in oil sands plants or in other energy supplies, might suggest to the United States that union would internalize this deficit and the capital flows necessary to develop the reserves.

The usual argument against this position is that a free-trade area will make Canada economically, and hence politically, stronger. However, although the manufacturing sector will be more efficient, it is difficult to argue that free trade, in itself, will produce a Canadian nation that is economically and politically stronger.

Of course, the vested interests of some groups in Canada and the United States may argue against union. Public interest in social security benefits, such as health care, which are more favorable in Canada than in the United States, may produce a strong wall of Canadian opposition to political union with the United States. Also, Canadian federally elected representatives and civil servants, fearful of what position they might hold in any larger entity, may prevent discussions from proceeding very far. Alternatively, U.S. authorities may prefer to try to extract the economic benefits they desire from Canada without having any responsibility for the long-run welfare of the populace itself and without having to accept free immigration of Canadians, which political union would imply. Other U.S. vested interests simply may not want strong voices from the north having a direct say in their affairs.

Sometimes much is made of how Sweden has survived, first in EFTA and more recently in access to the EEC, when it is but a small country facing the industrial might of countries such as

---

[29]See Susan Crean, *Who's Afraid of Canadian Culture?* (Don Mills, Ontario: General Publishing, 1976).

Germany.[30] Yet the fact is ignored that the Swedish have limited foreign participation in their productive resources and have developed powerful transnational corporations of their own. In 1965, for example, foreigners held only about 5 percent of Swedish industry, and since 1916, Sweden has had limited foreign ownership of natural resources and real property. Direct government participation, especially in mining, has also been extensive. In 1966, government firms accounted for 82 percent of employment in mining. Again, the Swedish have emphasized backward linkages·from mining to the development of electrical machinery, as well as generating equipment for the hydro-electric sector, and of mineral- and metal-working machinery.[31]

Again, the way that Ireland has been able to maintain its independence in spite of heavy trade with the United Kingdom, a common language, a currency tied to sterling, substantial migration of Irish to the United Kingdom, the fact that 70 percent of the transnational companies in Ireland are of U.K. origin, and free trade between them through the EEC has been cited as a good reason to expect that closer integration of the Canadian and U.S. economies will never result in political union of some sort.[32] However, the long history of cultural differences between Ireland and the United Kingdom and their continuing bitter disagreement over Ulster give a strong rationale for continuing Irish independence.[33]

In the Canadian-U.S. situation there are no such strong bases for disagreement. Moreover, given the strong nationalistic fervor of the United States and the minimal amount of such fervor that Canada generally displays, a free-trade area negotiated at this time, out of a position of comparative actual, or perceived, weakness on Canada's part, could well rekindle that old, smoldering American aspiration of one continental country — an aspiration in response to which Canada was initially established over 110 years ago. Canada could be swept into the U.S. vortex.

---

[30] Wonnacott, *op. cit.*, Chap. 12.

[31] Stockholm Enskilda Bank, *Some Data about Sweden, 1969-70* (Stockholm, 1969), pp. 35 and 87; Patricia Mohr, *Economic Development Strategies and Foreign Ownership Policies of Selected Countries*, Mineral Bulletin MR 123 (Ottawa: Energy, Mines and Resources Canada, 1972), pp. 13-18. See also Wilkinson, "L'impact d'une zone de libre-échange," *op. cit.*, pp. 485-86.

[32] Peyton Lyon, *Canada-United States Free Trade and Canadian Independence* (Ottawa: Economic Council of Canada, 1975), pp. 21-22.

[33] Lyon mentions these too but does not interpret them as distinguishing the United Kingdom-Ireland situation from the Canada-United States case.